HAPPY
COUPLES

HAPPY COUPLES

Julián Melgosa
Dean of the School of Education and Psycology,
Walla Walla College, College Place, Washington, USA
Ex-President of the School of Graduate Studies, AIIAS

Annette D. Melgosa
M.A. In Library and Information Studies
Associate librarian of Peterson Memorial Library

Safeliz

Title: Happy Couples
Authors: Julián Melgosa and Annette D. Melgosa
Original title in Spanish: Parejas felices

Abridged version of *To Couples. Enjoying a stable, lifelong relationship*

Project Coordination: Editorial Safeliz, S. L.
Cover image: Stock.xchng/Fotolia
Cover design: Bezalel&Aoliabe Design

Copyright by © Editorial Safeliz, S. L.
Pradillo, 6 · Pol. Ind. La Mina
E-28770 · Colmenar Viejo, Madrid, Spain
Tel.: [+34] 91 845 98 77 · Fax: [+34] 91 845 98 65
admin@safeliz.com · www.safeliz.com

April 2012: 1st edition
ISBN: 978-84-7208-421-6

IMP02

CONTENTS

1 The couple ... past and present

Chapter Summary

Silvia and Peter are married and have school-age twins. The school year has just started and the topic of conversation over dinner was very interesting. The children brought up the following topic:

"Today we counted how many children in our class haven't got a father or a mother and there are 15 out of the 25 of us." "That's impossible! All children have parents."

"Well, in our school, there are lots who don't have a father, some who don't have a mother and one with only a grandmother."

"Let's see. Tell us who those children are."

"Well. Nat lives with his mother and sees his father once a year because he lives abroad and sends them money."

"Elizabeth says the same. But her father doesn't give them any money."

"Then there's Hamid. His parents are foreign and his mother still hasn't come over. He lives with his father and his sisters. But he's been living like that for years."

"And Stella". Her parents are divorced and she lives with her mother and her stepfather who has two daughters. We tease her saying: 'Are your stepsisters like Cinderella's?' Her father has also remarried and lives a long way away."

"Max is the funniest. He says that aunts and uncles are better than parents, because parents are very strict. That's because Max lives with his parents, brothers and sisters, aunts, uncles and cousins. They must have a very big house or else they wouldn't all fit in!"

Today, marriage continues to be the option chosen by over 80% of those legally able to do so. Unfortunately marriages often fail, so the legitimate question arises: "What do we get married for?" "If a couple's aims can be met without legal, social or religious commitments, then why should we perpetuate this ancient institution?" "Why strive to leap over obstacles when it would be easier to avoid them in the first place?"

Arguments do exist in support of **committed legal marriage**s. Below are some of the strengths to be considered:

- A marital relationship generally implies a greater level of commitment, thus placing expectations on a more realistic plane than merely living together and **fostering greater effort which leads to greater stability**.

- When facing a crisis, the knowledge that marriage is a lasting commitment offers a couple **greater impetus to confront their difficulties**.

- A committed married couple **only contemplates splitting up in exceptional circumstances**, whilst unmarried couples often consider separation as an escape route to everyday difficulties.

- The **social environment** (relatives, friends, work colleagues and so on) tends to confer **higher expectations for stability** on a marital relationship, yet does not usually do so for freely associated couples.

- **Marriage is free of the social stigma** suffered by cohabiting couples. This factor has shown a significant decrease in liberal societies, but remains strong in the rest of the world.

- Many unmarried couples decide to marry after living together for years and even after having children. This shows that they themselves consider marriage to be a step forward, a state in which one **attains a higher level of commitment and stability**.

- When a marriage breaks up, **the law provides any children and the spouse awarded their custody, with financial support**. This is also true of common-law couples, but not for those who live together without any kind of legal registration.

So-called "cohabitation", in comparison to formal marriage, is a popular option today. It is argued that it is possible to live together and to obtain the same marital and family benefits as that of a married couple while counting on the same timeframe and sufficient freedom to do so. Nevertheless, it is over-simplistic to assess cohabitation in these terms. David Popenoe and Barbara Whitehead analyzed a large number of studies on this topic, providing the information included in the box above.

Furthermore, living together outside marriage or a common-law arrangement carries important **legal disadvantages**, especially in the case of separation or death. In these cases, verbal promises or agreements are of no consequence. Before the law, the couple has no legal tie and thus has no right to the corresponding legal protection.

Therefore, prior to starting a relationship of this kind, the following issues should be taken into consideration: goods acquired together; the last will and testament; the tutelage of underage children; the protection of the most vulnerable partner in the case of break-up and so on.

FROM THE PSYCHOLOGIST'S DESK "And now she wants to get married ..."

Clara and I met for the first time two years ago and we soon started going out together to get to know each other better. We've been living together for a year, but now Clara is not happy and wants us to get married. My question is: If everything is going well and we do not have any problems, why should we get married?

If everything is going well and you do not have any problems, why is Clara dissatisfied with the current situation? Your experience is very common among couples who live together with no legal tie. The man is often satisfied because the arrangement seems practical. However, most women see the situation as transitory, unstable and insecure.

Comparisons made between women who are in a cohabiting relationship and those in a conventional marriage have demonstrated that the former suffer more from depression and find their relationship less satisfactory. The results obtained are the same for couples with and without children.*

If you love Clara you should consider her suggestion seriously. If you do, you will contribute to her emotional well-being. Like many other women, she does not feel safe and secure in a relationship she feels is uncertain. And this feeling of dissatisfaction will grow with time, unless your relationship is formalized.

*Brown, Susan L. "The Effect of Union Type on Psychological Well-Being: Depression Among Cohabitors Versus Marrieds." *Journal of Health and Social Behavior* 41:241-155, 2000.

A balanced marriage is beneficial for both partners. Various comparative studies, especially those carried out by Linda Waite*, show that although it takes effort and sacrifice to maintain a marriage, there are very marked benefits:

Married partners ...

- **... enjoy a healthier life-style**. Life in a stable marriage is a factor in quality of life. This includes: better eating habits and physical exercise; less high risk behavior and a lower consumption of drugs and alcohol than bachelors, divorcees, widows or widowers.

- **... live longer**. Married partners live to a greater age than bachelors, divorcees, widows or widowers. The difference, which is of several years, is attributed to the improved level of emotional support enjoyed by stable couples.

- **... enjoy greater levels of sexual satisfaction**. 54% of married partners interviewed considered their sexual activity to be highly satisfactory, whilst that of cohabiting partners reached 44%. Levels of sexual satisfaction among bachelors, widows and widowers is still lower.

- **... have more material resources.** Married life tends to be economically more efficient and presents more opportunities to accumulate goods.

- **... foster better development in their children**. In general terms, children brought up in families with both their natural parents, obtain better academic grades, enjoy greater emotional stability and receive better care and attention than those brought up in broken homes or with unmarried parents. Furthermore, their parents' better economic standing enable the children access to a more extensive range of educational opportunities.

*Waite, L. y Gallagher, M. 'The case for marriage'. Cambridge, Massachussetts: Harvard University Press, 1999; Waite, L. "Does marriage matter?". *Demography*, 32:1995 (4), 483-507.

The many modes in which couples and families exist today may be due to wish to break out of established molds or to depart from blind tradition. However, we do not hear that the generalized tendency is one of living the life of a hermit, of wanting to isolate ourselves from all others and to have no close relationships. Very few people can be happy when alone. Our most enjoyable activities lose their attraction when they cannot be shared. A couple, made up of a man and a woman who are committed to each other, represents the ideal context in which to reach a **reasonable state of happiness**, within the imperfection in which we live.

Therefore, the vast majority of people, even in this time of changing values, seek the company of someone of the opposite sex and the legitimization of this relationship. The need to be united with someone who provides friendship, love, support and emotional balance is a universal phenomenon.

Marriage is a transcendental step, which should be taken for a reason. When there are very few reasons, this union runs the risk of breaking up. Below we have some valid reasons for marriage that should be taken into account by both parties in order to improve the probabilities of forging a successful marriage:

1. **Love**. We all need to love and be loved. A healthy marriage forms the ideal context in which to bring about that love. Yet, what is the meaning of love? Classical Greek refers to the concept of love in several ways (see the box on the page 12). One of them refers to the agape, a sublime love based on altruism. This is the fundamental underpinning for love and the basis of all types of love.

2. **Companionship**. People come together to have a companion at their side with whom they can share the enjoyable and painful moments of their lives; someone in whom they can confide the most hidden intimacies of their souls. This company precludes loneliness as well as the sadness and emotional instability which tends to rise when one lives alone.

3. **The need for self-realization**. Marriage forms an environment in which the couple can realize themselves and grow. It fosters the right kind of self-esteem, balanced habits and the most complete form of psychological well-being.

4. **Sharing sexuality**. Sexual needs of both men and women are better satisfied within the security of marriage. Although sex is not everything, it is an important part of married life that helps to maintain love and unity between both partners.

5. **Sharing parenthood**. Although having children brings with it added responsibilities, efforts, worries and frustrations, it is one of the greatest privileges conferred on mankind. Both men and women express a feeling of satisfaction when they become parents. The growth of the family establishes prolonged emotional ties between parents and children, which translate into a balanced state of mind.

Both the physical and emotional union of man and woman originated so long ago that they precede all historic record. They seem to be an inherent tendency and need in mankind. Both men and women want to complete their existence by forming a couple with a partner. History shows that marriage as an institution has existed in practically every culture.

As far as authority within the couple is concerned there are two basic forms:

- **Matriarchy**: Where it is the woman who possesses and exercises authority in the couple and the family.

- **Patriarchy**: Where the person possessing and exercising authority in the couple and the family is the man.

Matriarchy is less widespread than patriarchy, but is more common than it seems. Cultures which publicly subscribe to a model of male authority have a fundamentally matriarchal family life. Outwardly, they live with an image of the dominant, authoritarian husband. However, behind closed doors it is the wife who has the power.

The patriarchal model is shared by many sectors of the world's population, sometimes due to religious influences and sometimes because of social tradition. The man controls the important decisions and his authority is above that of his wife and children. This system has often given rise to the abuse of marital power leading to family violence, both of a physical and psychological nature.

Curiously, the Old Testament already starts to make reference to a balance in deciding power within the couple and to the place that should be made for divine power. Wise King Solomon illustrated it thus:

"Two are better than one, because they have a good reward for their toil. For if they fall, one will lift up his fellow; but woe to him who is alone when he falls and has not another to lift him up. Again, if two lie together, they are warm; but how can one be warm alone? And though a man might prevail against one who is alone, two will withstand him. A threefold cord is not quickly broken." (Ecclesiastes 4: 9-12). The highlighting is ours.

Why does the author speak of two yet at the end he mentions a three-strand cord? That third strand of the cord refers to the divine and supernatural power, supplementing what is not humanly possible. It is therefore fitting to invite the Creator to form an essential part of the life of a couple. This enhances their respect and love for each other and provides the necessary altruism for the couple to grow daily and for the compensations of married life to be more and more rewarding.

If we wish to go back to the oldest known reference to marriage and the family, we have to go to the first book of the Holy Scriptures and more precisely to the book of Genesis. It is there that we are told of the first couple and their origin.

Then the Lord God said, "It is not good that the man should be alone; I will make him a helper fit for him." [...]So the Lord God caused a deep sleep to fall upon the man, and while he slept took one of his ribs and closed up its place with flesh; and the rib which the Lord God had taken from the man he made into a woman and brought her to the man. Then the man said, "This at last is bone of my bones and flesh of my flesh; she shall be called Woman, because she was taken out of Man." Therefore a man leaves his father and his mother and cleaves to his wife, and they become one flesh. (Genesis 2: 18, 21-24).

The initiative of forming a couple as opposed to a unisex or asexual being belongs to God and not to man. Marriage is, therefore, an option proposed by God with a view to it

- being permanent,
- satisfying the human need to love and be loved,
- fostering companionship and friendship,
- satisfying mutual sexual needs,
- procreating,
- establishing a suitable environment for children's upbringing and development.

What is love?

Classical Greek has three terms for referring to what modern languages all gather together under the expression 'love'.

- **Eros**. This is the most primary form of love. It refers to an impulse-seeking sensual satisfaction. It is passionate love.
- **Fileo**. This refers to the love provided by a relationship based on emotional satisfaction. It could be used to refer to the love which fosters companionship and friendship as well as the ideal love for nature, knowledge or music.
- **Agape**. This is the highest representation of love. It occurs on principle and not on impulse. It is projected in the other, even when the other person corresponds to a lesser degree. It is the infallible love of a marriage relationship and the one which fosters other types of love. Paul, the Apostle, explained this supreme love to believers in Corinth 2,000 years ago in a letter which now forms part of the Holy Scriptures. The essence of this is outlined below:

Love is ...

- being patient
- being kind
- rejoicing in the truth
- long-suffering
- trusting
- tolerating
- even more important than faith
- even more important than hope
- long lasting

Love is not ...

- being envious
- being conceited
- being proud
- being rude
- being selfish
- getting angry
- being resentful
- rejoicing in wrong

(Read the complete text in the Bible: 1 Corinthians 13: 1-10)

2

Courtship

Chapter Summary

*E*stelle and Marius are making plans for their wedding in eight months' time. They have been going out together for two years. The outlook for this couple is very good: They possess similar values and ideals, a good level of communication, and skills in conflict-resolution; they are conscious of their own and other people's temperaments and are in relative agreement regarding their roles in their life together as a couple. Both consider marriage as binding for life as opposed to a civil contract which may be rescinded if they fall into difficulties.

Bridget and Alister represent a case which is substantially different. From the very beginning they were strongly attracted to each other and being together became more and more enjoyable; going for walks, to dances, on trips etc. They have been having a really good time. However, they have hardly talked about life as a couple, or the difficulties of getting used to married life. They have not discussed their new roles in their life together and they have not even talked about whether or not to have children.

In the second case, courtship has not been used as it should: As a preparation for marriage.

In the past, the choice of companion was a decision belonging to the young people's parents or relatives (see in chapter 1); whereas today, al-though this custom continues to exist in certain cultures, the free choice of friends that lead to courtship or marriage, now predominates.

What should we look for when choosing?

Everyone wants to marry the ideal person and therefore we look for certain features in our desired partner. The box on the previous page presents a series of attributes which serve as guidelines for those who have to make such a choice.

Choosing a partner can take place in several different ways. Whilst some experts highlight one process, others concentrate on another. But

there is wide consensus that the choice of spouse is determined by:

- similarity, having things in common;
- elimination or by discarding options;
- initial attraction;
- a combination of factors.

Similarity

After analyzing a broad sample of publications, David Olson, from the University of Minnesota and John Defrain from the University of Nebraska, established that people tend to choo-se a partner on the basis of similarity in age, social class, academic achievement, race and religion (see Olson, D.H. and Defrain, J. 2000).

By this we are not advocating that success lies in **complete homogeneity**. In fact, extreme similarity *brings the added issue of boredom*. Furthermore, differences can be an advantage. For example, in a couple where one partner is thrif-ty and the other a spendthrift, they may exert a mutual balancing effect, thus avoiding the extremes of meanness or squandering. Despite this, we must acknowledge that reaching such a balance can be rough, especially if the differences are numerous.

Elimination

In line with this perspective, those who are seeking a companion follow a process of *selection filters*.

Kerckhoff and Davis (Kerckhoff, A.C. and Davis, K.E. 27: 295-303, 1962) were the first to propose this elimination mechanism. They suggested five levels of filtering, through which options are eliminated until there is only a reduced number of possible partners.

1. Proximity

One chooses between people who are

nearby, available in time and place. Those who reside in big cities, with a wide circle of contacts and opportunities to travel, have more options open to them than those who live in smaller places and do not have the means to meet many people.

2. Social Group

Amongst those people available, some are immediately eliminated because they belong to a very different social sector. We are referring to those with a significant age difference or belonging to a social class which is neither accessible nor acceptable.

3. Physical attraction

Even among those who come from an acceptable group, there has to be some kind of mutual attraction to start the relationship off. Therefore, those whose level of attraction is less than satisfactory are also eliminated.

4. Compatibility

Having passed through the preceding filters, there must also be a certain compatibility in personality, interests, plans, values and so on between two potential partners.

5. Compensation

The last filter is based on compensation. Each candidate assesses what he or she will put into and receive from an eventual relationship. If the exchange is considered reasonable, they continue; if not, the relationship is not worthwhile and they go their separate ways.

Initial attraction

Another way of explaining how people choose a companion is using Murstein's theory (Murstein, B.I. 42: 777-792. 1987). This theory suggests three basic steps:

- A man and a woman feel attracted to each other, either because of their physical appearance or due to an inexact first impression which is termed stimulus. This is what is widely known as love at first sight. With-out this component the relationship is unlikely to gel.

- Once the stimulus or initial attraction has taken effect the couple assesses each other's values and how they complement each other. They compare the differences and similarities in their ways of thinking (politics, religion, ecology …), in their behavior (life-style, work, leisure …) and in planning the future (housing, children, parents, in-laws …).

- Finally they analyze the various functions or roles that one or other will carry out in their lives together. The potential partners will ask:
  - ✓ Who will be the main provider of our material needs?
  - ✓ Who will exercise most authority and in which areas?
  - ✓ If we have children, who will bring them up?
  - ✓ If we both work, how will we split the housework?

A combination of factors

It is evident that diverse viewpoints highlight different aspects and the answer is to learn from all of them.

The similarity theory is useful when it comes to explaining that people look for features in their future spouse which are similar to their own. It is also true, however, that many people look for what they feel is interesting in a man or a woman, independently of whether they share this characteristic or not.

The elimination theory establishes an order by which the sample number of potential candidates is reduced until partners make their respective choices. Whilst this mechanism is logical and true in general terms, there are many exceptions to this rule as love does not always follow a logical pattern.

The theory of initial attraction indicates a progression which is sometimes found and sometimes not. The idea of love at first sight does not exist in couples who have known each other since childhood and who then began going out to get to know each other better to eventually finish up happily married.

Bachelorhood

In the last instance there are those who do not find the right partner and remain unmarried. Others freely choose to stay single. Although most people choose marriage as their life-style, the advantages of remaining single are not to be disdained. Their level of autonomy and freedom are notably higher and this may be translated, especially when it is a situation adopted by choice, into a higher standard of living. They have to foster friendships and stay closer to their families to find affection. It can also be fulfilling for them to enter support groups and offer services to others by being a volunteer in an altruistic NGO for example, or collaborating with their church, political party etc.

GETTING READY FOR MARRIAGE

AREA QUESTIONS/ACTIVITIES

1. Expectations
- Make a list of eight specific things that you expect of your partner.
- Describe what you think a typical day will be like, from morning till night, after your honeymoon is over.

2. Communication
- How do you feel when you speak and he or she does not pay you any attention?
- When you are annoyed, how do you communicate with him or her?
- Are you afraid to share intimate thoughts with him or her?

3. Conflicts
- Make a list of four points which you disagree on.
- How do you face conflicts?
- How does your partner face them?
- Which is your favored style for overcoming conflict?
  - ✓ To win
  - ✓ To give away
  - ✓ To leave
  - ✓ To resolve

(you will find more information on conflict and how to resolve them in chapter 6 "Crisis within the couple") (The box on page 34 Signs of violence, describes the profile of a man incapable of resolving conflict in a civilized way.)

4. Personality
- Use 8 – 10 adjectives to describe your personality.
- Use 8 – 10 adjectives to describe your partner's personality.
- What features do you think you should tone down for the love of your partner?

5. Functions
- Who is the head of the household for you? What does being head of the household mean?
- In your family, what would you like the roles of the man and the woman to be?
- In your case, which of the two will be the primary breadwinner? What will the other do?
- Which member of the couple

AREA QUESTIONS/ACTIVITIES

will be in complete charge of the housework? How will the other partner collaborate in every-thing?

6. Finances
- Who will be responsible for economic matters in your marriage?
- When it comes to an important purchase, will you consult with your partner?
- Were you brought up in a household of plenty or in one where money was scarce? How will this affect your way of spending when married?
- Make up a hypothetical list of monthly expenditures for when you are married. Write down the most necessary items first.

7. Sexuality
- On a scale of 0 – 10 indicate how important you rate sex within marriage.
- How often would you want to make love?
- Are you willing to talk openly about your expectations regarding sex?
- What is the best family planning method? What do you think is your partner's opinion regarding this method?

8. Children
- Would you like to have children? How many?
- How do you think having children would change your life-style?
- What would be your responsibilities and what would your partner's be in the care and upbringing of your children?

9. Leisure
- Hat is your favorite free-time activity? Does it fit in with your partner's t preferences?
- How much do you think you will be able to compromise to accommodate his or her preferences?
- If you did not reach a consensus, how would you feel if part of his

AREA QUESTIONS/ACTIVITIES

or her leisure was spent with other people?

10. In-laws and family
- ow important to you are the relationships with your respective families?
- Which of the two of you do you think is responsible for these relationships?
- Would you give up some of your family holidays to deepen relations with your in-laws?
- When your parents get older, who will be responsible for their care and attention?
- When your partner's parents get older, who will be responsible for their care and attention?

11. Values and beliefs
- Assess from 0 (total disagreement) to 10 (total agreement) the amount of consensus between your partner and yourself in questions of values and beliefs.
- Which are the areas of values and beliefs where you differ most?
- Do you profess the same religion?
- If YES, are there significant differences in how important religion is for each of you? How do you think faith will affect your daily lives?
- If NO, do you foresee that this difference could lead to problems or conflict? And if you have children, what religious instruction do you think they should receive?

12. The unexpected
- How would you react in the event of the following in your marriage?
- You discover you cannot have children.
- Your partner falls seriously ill.
- Job loss.
- Having to move to lower quality accommodation.
- Experiencing major economic difficulties.
- Death of a child.
- Discovering your partner is unfaithful to you.

These questions should first be answered separately and then responses should be compared to establish an open dialog. Many of the questions may require expert advice from a specialist or someone with a long experience of marriage. Do not hesitate to seek advice concerning how to face these problems.

Getting to know each other better and preparing oneself for marriage are highly transcendental tasks for both partners. In most cultures great importance is placed on the wedding ceremony and everything this involves. Be it due to family and social pressure or for the joy of realizing a fantasy held for many years, enormous sums of money and many hours of work are spent in planning a wedding. It is estimated that most weddings cost the equivalent of half of a family's yearly income at the very least. This includes the cost of invitations, clothes, the ceremony, the reception, photographs, the honeymoon and a list of miscellaneous items. If we think of the time spent, we find that many weddings take up to one year to plan. During this period, there are many exciting moments but there are also times full of stress and anxiety.

Unfortunately, in many cases little effort is made in getting to know each other better and preparing oneself, not for the wedding, but for life together afterwards.

Preparation for marriage should be intentional and to a certain extent, **organized and systematized**. This can be done independently, with the couple devoting some time to broadly discuss a list of relevant topics concerning marriage. On other occasions dialog is brought about through organizations which offer **premarital courses**. The dynamics of such courses vary according to their programs:

a. Some use lectures and talks to listeners about marital problems and their possible prevention and solution.

b. Other more sophisticated ones include psychological exploration by means of **personality tests** with individual sessions in which an expert offers advice tailored to each couple, on the basis of the test results.

c. Others aim to initiate participants in the task of **good communication**. Plenary sessions are reduced to a minimum and couples are given the opportunity to talk privately about their issues and problems.

SIGNS OF VIOLENCE

One of the most pressing problems is violence within the couple or the family. It is common to find high levels of family abuse in all societies, even in the most wealthy and civilized. Below we have a list of violence indicators which already appear during courtship and may be clear precursors to an abusive relationship. Examine this list and check to see if they are present in your partner:

- He or she drinks alcohol regularly.
- He or she is insensitive towards animals or children.
- He or she says hurtful or humiliating things to you.
- He or she wants to control what you do, say, buy and so on.
- He or she wants to separate you from your family, friends or work companions.
- He or she has very marked mood swings.
- He or she has behaved violently in the past although always with excuses.
- When you desagree he or she grabs and shakes you.
- When angry he or she throws or breaks things or bangs his or her fists down on the table.
- He or she blames other people for his or her problems.

If you have regularly witnessed in your partner any of the indicators in this list, you may run the risk of becoming a victim of household violence. The more indicators that are present, the greater the risk you run. It might be sensible to get out of this relationship in time.

We may say that one's temperament is not an impediment for making a good contribution to courtship or marriage. The many-sided human community always needs all of them. Nevertheless *it is useful to know the strengths and weaknesses in each other's temperament to find out if they are clearly incompatible.*

This point can be fundamental when living together and, therefore, it is a good idea for a good psychologist to run temperament **tests on the couple**, and then to act in consequence. We must not forget that temperament, being the physiological prevalence of an organic system, is in the main product of inheritance. It is therefore not easily molded like character and should not be confused. Our temperament is as it is and we cannot expect our partner to change it very substantially. *It can be tempered but not changed.* Thus the importance of identifying it beforehand.

Our interpersonal relations are greatly affected by temperament. *It is therefore necessary for both partners to have an idea of each other's temperamental tendencies* in order to be forewarned of their strengths and weaknesses.

The first theory regarding temperament was devised by **Hippocrates**. He thought that in the human body the domination of one fluid over all the others led to one or ano-ther kind of temperament. Today that concept has changed, but Hippocrates' nomenclature for temperaments is still used today: Sanguine, choleric, melancholic and phlegmatic.

Temperament is defined as a person's particular way of reacting to circumstances in life. This kind of reaction is brought about by the physiological prevalence of an organic system such as the nervous, circulatory or muscular systems. The box covering the next two pages describes the most outstanding features of the four kinds of temperament and their **virtues**. Their **negative points** are also described together with the most desirable aims as far as **changes** are concerned, since these adverse aspects may be tempered.

The description offered by the Apostle, Paul, is not only applicable to love between a man and a woman but also to any situation. In fact, Paul's text has been and still is considered the account of ideal love, built on 15 elements.

Love ...

- **... is patient**. Love is a great source of satisfaction, but love for another may also call for patience.
- **... is kind**. Love is full of good will, with no ulterior motives and the clear wish of doing good to the other.
- **... has no envy**. Far from intending rivalry and avarice, true love finds satisfaction and not sadness in the triumph of an opponent.
- *... is not boastful*. He who enjoys true love does not boast, does not look to stand out, but rather to make the other happy.
- **... is not conceited**. Love is not compatible with vanity, as vanity can make the other feel inferior.
- **... does nothing improper**. The conduct of one who loves is correct and considerate. It does nothing out of place.
- **... seeks nothing for itself**. He who loves truly strives to do good to the other, more than for himself.
- **... is not irritable**. Being well-mannered and never losing one's temper are indicators of respect and true love.
- **... is not resentful**. In every couple there are faults which should be discussed, forgiven, and forgotten, never to be brought up again.
- **... does not rejoice in wrong, but in the truth.** A loving relationship must be open, honest and fair; a context which precludes lying.
- **... is long-suffering**. This coincides in part with the first characteristic, adding here that a loving relationship includes tolerance for all things.
- **... is trusting**. A true loving relationship requires trust in the other and accepting his words and conduct as sincere.
- **... is hopeful**. Love does not consist of a state of perfection, but rather one of hopes and ideals which are fulfilled from day to day.
- **... bears all**. For the third time we find the importance of long-suffering or bearing possible difficulties in a loving relationship.
- **... is everlasting**. Although love between a man and woman may die out, the love proposed by Paul lasts throughout life.

TEMPERAMENT

Sanguine

Virtues

Those with a sanguine temperament appear to enjoy life more than the other three kinds. They are sociable, talkative, always laughing and in a good mood. In a couple, a sanguine partner fosters an optimistic, affable and continually happy relationship. They can easily forget past insults and are ready to forgive or ask for forgiveness.

Defects

Many of their defects come from their absentmindedness: They forget their friends and their commitments, they are easily distracted from their obligations … . This can bring about problems in a relationship as loved ones want to be shown they are loved with small gestures, anniversary surprises etc. They also tend to monopolize the conversation and to concentrate on themselves, listening very little, thus building an important barrier in a loving relationship. Their impulsiveness leads them to often make mistakes as they do not stop to think of the consequences of their acts or words.

Aims for a better relationship between the couple

- Develop good habits in terms of loving gestures.
- Try to be more sensitive to a partner's feelings.
- Be more dependable and respect commitments; be more serious when so required.
- Foster self-discipline in the life shared with a partner.
- Strive to speak less and listen more.
- Try to be truly humble and avoid letting egocentricity prevail.

Choleric

Virtues

People with a choleric temperament have enormous will-power and security that lead them to great achievements. They enjoy huge reserves of energy to fulfill their objectives. Within the couple they are useful as they are good leaders, capable of managing things in order to reach a better situation.

Defects

In choleric people, reason is so dominant that they tend to be implacable, merciless and insensitive. This can be problematic in a couple's life together, where they can hurt the others' feelings by their coldness or lack of emotion. Within a relationship, they do no let themselves be led by the other, but rather they try to take charge and be the absolute leader.

Aims for a better relationship between the couple

- Strive to be warmer and more human with the other.
- Recognize how easily they lose their temper and exercise control over this impulse.
- Ask for forgiveness and recognize their mistake when they have made one.
- Share decision-making with the loved one.
- Leave perfectionism on one side and try to be more flexible in their shared life.

Melancholic

Virtues

Melancholic people are sensitive by nature and capable of reaching a thorough understanding of others. This does not impede them taking action or solving problems. They are cautious and reflexive in their way of thinking. They like things to be done well. In their life with a partner they assume full responsibility for planning and attention to detail, and they show their companions loyalty, sacrifice and commitment.

Defects

Their analytical and observant minds often lead them to examine the facts and their implications from all sides which may sometimes provoke fear and anxiety. Melancholic people tend to be pessimistic and apprehensive. With their partners they can become distrustful, reading non-existent intentions into words and acts. They also tend to be perfectionists and expect perfection from the other, although not with the same force as a choleric person. Even when they may present a calm and peaceful picture on the surface, inside they may be experiencing feelings of rejection or shame which, unlike choleric people, they are unable to reveal but rather they keep to themselves.

Aims for a better relationship between the couple

- Avoid being critical and pessimistic with a partner.
- Trust in a loved one's good intentions.
- Practice looking to the future with a partner, calmly and with confidence.
- Use time in the service of others rather than in self contemplation.
- Recognize and be sincerely appreciative of a partner's achievements.

Phlegmatic

Virtues

Capable of keeping calm even in the most adverse of situations, phlegmatic people contribute to maintaining balance and peace within their partner relationship. They are kind, pacifying and diplomatic. They also possess a very important quality for life within a couple: They know how to listen. And as a result, they tend to be good counselors.

Defects

The slowness and apparent lack of enthusiasm may make others shun them. This may constitute a problem for many professional tasks. Within the couple, their excessively irritating calm and slowness sometimes try their partners' patience. Phlegmatic people have little self-confidence thus making them indecisive and lacking in motivation. They easily fall into sarcasm to mock those who bother, or alternatively they adopt a standoffish attitude.

Aims for a better relationship between the couple

- Overcome passiveness toward a loved one.
- Strive to add rhythm to one's activities.
- Show deep respect toward a companion.
- Acknowledge one's insecurity and rise above it to attain a better relationship.

Going into marriage without having a good idea of male and female **biology** and **psychology** represents a serious risk. If there were ever a compulsory course for partners preparing for marriage, one of the first topics would be the **differences** between men and women.

Differences of biological nature

- **The locomotive system**, for example, performs differently in men and in women because their muscle and bone structures are different.

- Their **stomachs**, **kidneys**, **liver** and **lungs** show important differences in size.

- The **blood circulation** in a woman is faster and her breathing is slower than in a man.

- If we talk of **endocrine glands**, the differences are not only quantitative but also qualitative. Let's take the female thyroid, for instance: This organ is especially active and produces physiological

differences (e.g. a skin tissue which is different to that of a man) and psychological differences (e.g. more intensely emotional than men).

- Even the blood has different compositions: a *woman's* blood has 20% fewer red blood cells, which makes her *more vulnerable to short-term tiredness.*

Differences of a psychological nature

There are also important phychological differences in ways of thinking and in conduct.

Although this phenomenon may be partly due to the influence of society, there are hormonal and constitutional reasons associated to differences in conduct.

- During lactation, differences can be seen between babies. Boys pay more attention to objects and toys, whereas girls pay attention to **people**.

- Boys use their **hands** more and **verbalize** less.

- Multiple studies on **aggressiveness** show consistently higher levels in boys than in girls.

- Girls learn to **speak and to write** earlier than boys, but they are overtaken by the latter in tasks **relating to time and space**, such as map reading or imagining objects in movement.

Falling in love is an emotional reaction, and as such it happens intensely in adolescence and youth. Experience has shown that the love felt may be real or merely a very intense but passing attraction. Below are some features to help differentiate between these two feelings:

True love ...

- ... overcomes the test of time, while attraction is only temporary and relatively fleeting.

- ... overcomes the test of separation. When, due to circumstances, the couple has to be apart for weeks or even months, their love goes on and grows, whilst attraction fades when one is separated from the other.

- ... brings positive results with it: Higher levels of academic achievement or performance at work and so on, whilst simple attraction tends to be associated with lower performance levels or negative results.

- ... fosters respect for the other regarding the physical aspects of the relationship, whereas attraction quickly moves on to sexual relations.

- ... acknowledges reality, the weak and the strong points, whereas attraction is blind and lacks any balanced judgment.

- ... tends to enjoy the approval of family and friends, whilst simple attraction does not.

The high emotional charge of love between a man and a woman should also, to a certain extent, have a logical and rational component which balances the progress of the relationship and avoids extremes.

All partners would like to have certain guarantees that their future married life will work out well. A profusion of data over the last 25 years, especially that coming from the "Prepare" program, provides us with clear results as to which factors give rise to a happy marriage (Fowers, B.J. and Olson, D.H. 12: 403-413. 1986; Larsen, A.S. and Olson D.H. 15:311-322. 1989). Using this information partners may assess their situation and be forewarned regarding future marital problems.

Below we have the seven most important factors in the success of a couple's life together:

1. Realistic expectations

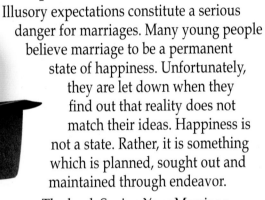

Illusory expectations constitute a serious danger for marriages. Many young people believe marriage to be a permanent state of happiness. Unfortunately, they are let down when they find out that reality does not match their ideas. Happiness is not a state. Rather, it is something which is planned, sought out and maintained through endeavor.

The book Saving Your Marriage Before It Starts by Les and Leslie Parrot, 1996, presents **four myths concerning marriage** which are a serious danger, especially for newlyweds:

• "When we marry we will not have great differences."

• "When we marry the good times will multiply."

• "When we marry the bad times will disappear."

• "When we marry my partner will make up for my defects."

All of these may happen, but it is not a mathematical conclusion, nor will it come about effortlessly. Both parties must devote time and dedication to cultivating love. It is true that marriage puts mechanisms in place that support a relationship, but it is not a magic formula that automatically resolves everything.

2. Good communication

The ability to communicate beyond merely daily information (e.g. the exchange of feelings and emotions) always appears amongst the first two or three success factors heading the lists. The vast majority of couples who consider themselves happy are satisfied with the way they communicate with their spouses. In a study in which more than twenty thousand couples took part (Olson, D.H., Fye,S. and Olson, A. 1999), it was confirmed that most of those who had identified themselves as happy couples, answered yes to questions like those below:

• "Are you satisfied with the way you chat together?"

• "Does your spouse make edifying (and not derogatory) comments towards you?"

• "Do you feel comfortable when asking your spouse what you want?"

• "Is it easy for you to express your feelings to your companion?"

The majority of couples considering themselves dissatisfied, answered no to these questions.

3. Conflict-resolving capacity

Due to the broad range of experiences before marriage and the multitude of personal ways of being and thinking, certain conflicts are inevitable in married life. The solution does not consist in trusting that friction, quarrels or disagreements will not occur. The solution is knowing how to resolve these situations. This is such an important topic that we have devoted a whole chapter, chapter 6, to learning marital conflict-solving models.

4. Liking a partner's personality

Another factor of fundamental importance is to like and admire a partner's way of being. The more features we admire in our partner, the more solid a foundation we have for our life together. And, this admiration *must be expressed in words* of praise toward a spouse to feed back into his or her self-esteem as a basic step towards a successful marriage.

Naturally there will be some

features in our partner that we do not like. Features such as stubbornness, dominance, jealousy, emotional instability or lack of punctuality are deeply rooted in some people, and we should understand that they are unlikely to disappear after the wedding. However, with effort and perseverance they can become weaker and both parties can get used to the change.

5. Ethical values and common religions

Religion and ethics appear as highly important values in securing a couple's stability. When there is consensus in these matters, the bond between two people is deeply strengthened, since their beliefs and convictions are not only in their minds but reach out to practically every aspect of human existence: from how they use their money to their dealings with others.

According to studies carried out on this topic (see Stinnett, N., Defrain, J. and Defrain, N., 1997), successful couples and families usually share similar religious and ethical convictions. On the other hand, lack of shared beliefs may be the direct cause of serious and dangerous arguments.

FROM THE PSYCHOLOGIST'S DESK

«He says it is time to make love»

I am 18 years old and I have been going out with my twenty-year-old boyfriend for three months. In general our relationship is good. I love him and he loves me. We go out at weekends and go for walks, dancing or to a show. We have a really good time together. However, now he is annoyed because he says it is time for us to make love and I do not agree. He insists: "If you love me, prove it to me in this way, or if not we should split up." For me the correct thing is to do this when we are married, but I believe I will lose my boyfriend if I do not let him. What should I do?

It is your right not to have sexual relations until after you are married and you should not give in just because he threatens you with breaking up. From your description it appears that your courtship is in its very early stages. You go out together to have fun. But you are not planning a serious, long-term relationship with common aims and considering marriage as your possible target. Your relationship is not at the right moment for making love. If your plans are to go on, tell him so; explain to him that you would like to take your relationship further and make wedding plans, and that you would like him to look at your future together in the same way. His reaction will immediately tell you if his thoughts are as serious as yours.

6. Agreement on each partner's responsibilities

The division of responsibilities and roles in married life is one of the greatest stumbling blocks in the lives of newlyweds. It should there-fore form part of any marriage preparation program. The question of whether both spouses are going to work needs to be discussed. If both choose to work outside the home, it is necessary to define which of the two jobs will be more important, something essential if a transfer were to be accepted. And if children are planned, there is also the need to define the respective roles of the father and the mother in their care and upbringing. Other lesser, but nonetheless important, decisions concern the car, the cleaning of the house, the washing and ironing or the cooking. These questions were easily addressed in the past because of the inflexibility of the roles in the couple, but today they are complex and require large doses of "give and take" to reach a satisfactory agreement. The test included (see page 16) enables couples to assess their level of mutual agreement, to act accordingly and make timely adjustments.

7. Agreement on how to employ free time

Our current life-style allows us more free time than a century ago when work both inside and outside of the home was much more intense. This advance engenders the risk of clashes when it comes to how free time should be employed. It is also necessary to explore this topic: "What are your favorite activities'" "What are yours?" "What changes might I make to match some of my preferences to his (or hers)?" The agreement need not be absolute but both parties should feel reasonably satisfied with the outcome.

INVALID REASONS FOR GETTING MARRIED

Marriages frequently spin out of control and may end in divorce because they were entered upon for the wrong reasons, for example:

- *Getting married as an act of rebellion*. There are parents who express dogmatic opinions on their idea of a suitable companion for their children. Some young people react to this by deciding to marry the very person who is rejected by their parents.

- *Getting married because of physical attraction*. Attraction as the only criterion for marriage is a risk because it is a short-lived phenomenon. If a marriage is built on the beauty of its partners, it will only last as long as this beauty continues and will deteriorate over the years. But even while it does continue, it is not enough to keep love alive.

- *Getting married out of pity*. There are cases where men or women cannot break off a relationship because of the hurt it would cause their partner, or there are those who marry to help a partner out of a problem (for example an addiction to alcohol). Compassion is no substitute for love and such marriages usually only last a short time.

- *Getting married for money*. When economic improvement is the only attraction, omitting all other criteria for living toge-ther, money is not enough to solve the problems which will arise in the relationship.

- *Getting married as an escape route*. Young people swallowed up in adverse family situations may see marriage as a fitting way out. For others it may represent emancipation from parents with whom they get on badly. Although wanting to escape such situations is a licit desire, it is dangerous to do so through marriage.

- *Getting married on the rebound*. When a relationship breaks up, there is sometimes a tendency to start another relationship and rush into marriage. This may be done out of spite or to relieve the hurt brought about by the separation. Neither of these are valid reasons for establishing a life-long relationship.

Although many marriages that began for the wrong reasons may result in happy relationships, we should bear in mind the high risk incurred by going into a marriage that is not based on love, but only and exclusively on one of the reasons outlined above.

Courtship should last a reasonable time; it should be neither too short nor too long. Overly-short courtships are associated with a high likelihood of divorce. Such courtships do not enable relationships to be founded within a framework of sufficiently mature knowledge about each other to make a sound decision about marriage. Generally, the decision to marry is based on their first romantic and artificial contact which does not represent the future spouses' real-life situation. On the other hand, overly-long courtships may bring about a deterioration in the relationship. Courtships which continue beyond the point of decision-making maturity, lose sight of the reasons behind courtship and lose their raison d'être.

Each courtship is different, but the majority follow a similar developmental process. The most notable stages are detailed below:

- **The affective stage**. This first stage in courtship is usually accompanied by a strong sense of predominantly physical attraction, and behavior is limited to superficial aspects. Conversations revolve around the partner's marvelous qualities. The couple enjoys just being together. Rarely are there arguments. This stage convinces young people that they were born for each other, but this first love does not guarantee a lasting love (see the box on page 19). Also at this stage, there may be demands from one party which are not shared by the other (see the box "From the Psychologist's Desk: 'He says it is time to make love'", on page 24).

- **The common objectives stage**. Once over the first stage, the depth of mutual analysis increases to the point of reaching sufficient knowledge to evaluate if the relationship may be directed towards a stable and definitive marriage. During this stage the couple observes each other's personality, tastes, values and attitudes. In this advanced period, partners observe any insurmountable hurdles that may lead to a break up or differences that can be negotiated.

- **The commitment stage**. If the courtship continues, it enters a phase which implies a firm, mutual commitment which generally translates into wedding plans. During this stage important problems often arise, sometimes to do with the wedding plans themselves, and others concerning personal issues (conflicts, fights etc.). It is good to consider this as some-thing normal during this stressful period. During these moments it is necessary for both parties to renounce some of their habits or attitudes to reach a situation whereby neither of the two is dominant.

- **Or breaking up**. Sometimes relationships do not thrive as they should and the best option is to break up altogeather. It is important to recognize the tensions caused by planning a wedding create clashes and upsets. Nevertheless this should not be a reason for breaking up a relationship. How-ever, the loss of love by one of the parties, clearly shown by what he or she says and does, is a good reason for breaking up. Other serious and important problems such as physical or psychological violence, and drug or alcohol abuse are sufficient indicators to break off a relationship. It is not advisable to continue with a courtship under the false hope that these serious problems will be remedied once one is married. The likelihood of a solution is very low, and the risks extreme.

3

Newlyweds

Chapter Summary

Rachel and Alan have been married for a little over a year. It has been a happy and satisfying period for them, although there have been some rough times which, fortunately, they have successfully overcome. At first their different lifestyles clashed, but little by little they have adapted to the new situation, especially as they know they come from families with very different backgrounds. Both try to be tolerant with the quirks of the other and they have made a commitment to pay more attention to each other's virtues than to their defects.

Initially, one of the sources of conflict was the division of responsibilities. Both are in full-time, paid employment. Rachel had expected that, when they got home from work, both of them would do the housework, but Alan refused to get involved as he considered this to be the work of women. This provoked several confrontations, but following dialog and negotiated agreements, the housework was shared between them and the problem was finally resolved.

Several months on, they had assimilated their respective needs and expectations.

The wedding night

After the wedding day comes the wedding night. Tradition places a lot of importance on this first night of a marriage. However, it should not be considered crucial as it comes after what is for many, the busiest day of their lives. There is, therefore, the likelihood that the wedding night is not the best example of closeness, tenderness and full sexual enjoyment. For this reason, here are a series of thoughts to bear in mind:

- **Do not place too much importance on this night**. From a "technical" viewpoint, this first night is unlikely to be successful because the newlyweds are tired and supposedly inexperienced. Nevertheless, success from the affective point of view is guaranteed.

- **Avoid selfishness from the outset.** Mutual affection and understanding are fundamental to make this experience one to look back on with pleasure.

- **Understand that skillfulness improves with time**. It is important not to feel let down by the outcome of this first night. Practice and time will lead to a much more satisfying sexual relationship.

- **For him: Be gentle and avoid roughness**. Being over-passionate may disconcert or be painful for her. It is therefore necessary to be as careful and affectionate as possible.

- **For her: Be composed and relaxed**. If she is a virgin (the ideal situation), a woman should not approach this night believing that sex will be painful. In fact, this will make intercourse more difficult. Neither should she worry if she finds a small amount of blood in her vagina, as this is totally normal.

An unforgettable honeymoon

The honeymoon is a rewarding occasion in its own right, and at the same time it affords a couple the opportunity to try out their new married life in a **relaxed atmosphere, away from** their normal environment. All in all, it is an opportunity to start off married life on the right foot. Planning the best honeymoon implies covering a few basic points which are outlined below:

- **Make plans well ahead of time**. A well-ordered honeymoon requires thorough preparation and this usually takes time, especially if dates and destinations fall in high season.

- **Make a joint decision regarding the choice of destination**. Although there are those who prefer

The Creator-Man-Woman

Experience has irrefutably shown that couples who believe in God, who count on Him and who maintain a living faith, show higher rates of stability than those who lack this transcendental spiritual base. The reason for this is the imbalance caused by a lack of equilibrium between the four dimensions present in man: The physical, the mental, the social and the spiritual dimensions. Neglect of any one of these breaks the balance of life.

Creator

Man

Woman

The honeymoon is a period in which the most beautiful and pleasurable aspects of courtship are intensified. What is of interest is getting away from everyday life, rather than trips which can tire a couple out. They need time and peace and quiet to concentrate on their feelings and to express them naturally.

to prepare their honeymoon alone in order to surprise their spouse, we recommend that plans be made jointly, thus getting to know each other's tastes and preferences.

- **Organize it according to the couple's tastes and not that of third parties**. This is a very meaningful occasion for the newlyweds and should be organized for their enjoyment rather than to impress others.

- **Avoid organized trips with too many activities**. Whilst on honeymoon, the couple want to be alone together, and so booking a busy tour with a lot of other people is not the most suitable arrangement. The aim of a honeymoon is to enjoy each other's company, without too many comings and goings.

- **Be prepared to encounter unknown details**. Living together, even in an unusual situation such as a

honeymoon, will mean finding out little things one does not like (peculiarities, untidiness, excessive tidiness, lack of cleanliness …). These should be discussed with tact and affection. On the other hand there will also be pleasant surprises which should be valued positively.

- **Be prepared for coming back to reality**. The honeymoon is soon over and it should be remembered that it is followed by a return to work and everyday obligations. It is the moment to prepare oneself mentally for the challenge that this adaptation will imply, and to which we have devoted most of this chapter.

- **Love: The best technique**. Above every intention, plan or activity, it should be remembered that the key to success for these special days resides in loving each other.

One of the first realities for a newlywed couple is to agree on the division of roles and responsibilities. This should be carried out in a climate of consensus.

The solution is to seek answers together for the following questions:

- Who, if not both of us, is going to work outside the home?
- Who will be responsible for finances?
- Who will do the shopping, cooking, and the washing-up?
- Who will keep the house clean and tidy?
- Who will wash and iron the clothes?
- Who will drive the car and be in charge of its maintenance?
- Who will carry out household repairs?
- If we have children, who will look after them?

A systematic way of doing this consists of *identifying each and every one of the tasks and responsibilities* necessary for each couple and negotiating until both are reasonably happy with the outcome. The box entitled "*How much do I take part?*" on the following page presents an inventory of responsibilities, which may be useful for starting up discussions of this kind.

This problem is simplified considerably when only one spouse works outside the home. Sometimes, especially when there are young children, it is not worthwhile keeping two jobs because of the additional costs that this implies.

In any case, in order to determine each spouse's areas of responsibility it is necessary to consider the following basic principles:

1. **Understand the wife's position**. Besides identifying the responsibilities of both partners, the couple should also have a very clear idea of where authority and decision-making are based. In most societies, women have been relegated to a secondary role. Nowadays, they participate more when decisions are taken.

Continued on page 32

«Who is responsible?» This is one of the questions in need of a clear answer before starting a marriage project. Therefore, it is necessary to discuss these tasks in detail and to reach agreements which satisfy both parties.

Instructions:

Use two copies of this inventory and fill them out separately. Once completed, compare your answers. Celebrate the points of agreement and take note of the points of disagreement, especially those which diverge by over 20 points. Negotiate these topics with your partner until a consensus is reached. Listen to alternative positions with the highest respect.

Him %	AREA OF RESPONSIBILITY	Her %
	EMPLOYMENT	
	1. Participation in paid employment	
	2. The importance of his job	
	3. The importance of her job	
	HOUSEWORK	
	1. Doing the shopping	
	2. Cooking	
	3. Washing the dishes	
	4. Cleaning the house	
	5. Tidying the house and its furnishings	
	6. Doing the washing	
	7. Ironing	
	8. Household repairs and maintenance	
	9. Household decorating	
	CHILDREN	
	1. Dressing them	
	2. Feeding them	
	3. Supervising homework and speaking to school teachers	
	4. Taking them to school	
	5. Buying their clothes	
	6. Putting them to bed	
	7. Playing with them	
	8. Disciplining them/teaching them values	

Him %	AREA OF RESPONSIBILITY	Her %
	OUTDOORS	
	1. Taking out the garbage	
	2. Looking after the yard	
	3. Vehicle cleaning and maintenance	
	MONEY	
	1. Making out the budget	
	2. Deciding on important purchases	
	3. Managing the bank account, payments and credit cards	
	VARIOUS	
	1. Planning holidays and activities as a family/couple	
	2. Attention and care of parents	
	3. Relationships with extended family	

Continued from page 30

2. **Understand the meaning of being head of the family**. To exercise leadership implies making decisions which benefit both partners, not those "which suit me". This is the surest way of exercising responsibility in marriage. The leader is the first ..., the first to serve.

3. **Reach strictly private agreements**. When newlyweds reach a consensus, it should be based on their personal criteria. The couple should establish their agreements in their own way and not necessarily follow what is normal among their families, friends or neighbors.

4. **Maintain a supporting, love-based attitude**. Any division of jobs will show some deficiencies. Therefore, it is necessary for the couple to have a positive attitude and support for each other. Housework may get out of hand, especially when there are small children at home. Mutual support may become necessary.

5. **Try to be flexible**. Rotating housework and other responsibilities may not only be useful but can also be fun, and furthermore, it will allow us to better understand our partner's perspective. There are men who cannot be left alone because they cannot cook and women who suffer an anxiety attack when faced with a flat tire ...

Sex is an **essential component** for the success of a couple. The happiest couples ...

- are satisfied and fulfilled in their sex lives;
- ensure that their companion uses sex fairly;
- trust their partner to be faithful;
- state that the other's interest in sex is acceptable.

On the other hand, most couples with serious problems in their lives together, find their sexual relations unsatisfactory.

It is therefore of utmost importance to begin married life with a good understanding of what sexuality is, and what it implies for a couple's happiness.

The first attempt to carry out research into the sex act was by **Masters and Johnson**. Their research, although now several decades old, is still valid in many respects. These sexologists proposed that a **complete sexual experience** comprised **four typical phases**, both in men and in women (see Masters, W.H. and Johnson, V.E. 1966). The table on pages 34-35 describes these phases of the sex act.

Some advices for a good sexuality

1. Adapting to a partner's specific needs

Acknowledging the vast sexual differences between men and women is fundamental in order for both partners to better understand each other's needs. A man can come home tired after a day at work, watch television, read the newspaper and not exchange a word with his wife and be ready to

make love when it is time for bed. The mechanism which precedes the sex act is very different for a woman. She needs to approach her husband progressively and emotionally (not just physically).

2. Discussing the topic openly

Jokes are often made about some aspects of sex, but **talking seriously about this topic** is not so frequent, even between a married couple. The best way to discover a companion's attitudes and preferences is to talk about it. The choice of the ideal moment and a romantic setting are important for this discussion. Avoid blaming or demanding, and send messages in the first person instead of recriminating your spouse. Below are some of our suggestions for starting off this discussion:

- What can I do to satisfy you when we have sex together?
- What can you do to satisfy me when we have sex?
- What do I feel when you respond to my sexual desire? And when you do not?
- How important for me is preparation for sex?
- How often would we like to make love?
- At what point in our sexual relation do I feel closest to you?

3. Preparing for Sex

All sexologists agree that **better lead-up** produces **greater satisfaction** for both spouses. This lead-up involves being kind and affectionate, using words and gestures to indicate mutual admiration and preparing the setting, all before any physical contact takes place.

4. Making a sexual encounter something more than copulation

Devote time to *foreplay* (kisses and caresses) and do not rush into intercourse. Most experts indicate **a minimum of twenty minutes** of sensual activities (for example, caresses, kisses, massages ...) before reaching intercourse. And this should be prolonged as long as both are enjoying this part of the encounter.

SEXUAL INTERCOURSE PHASES

PHASE	MALE

1. Excitement Phase

The presence of external stimuli (such as kisses, caresses…) or internal (the memory of a prior sexual encounter…) produces a series of physical and psychological variations which unleash the process of sexual excitement.

1. Excitement Phase

In the male the most powerful signals for excitement are visual in nature. It is therefore easier to excite a man with pictures or erotic gestures. Memories and tactile stimuli also produce this excitement, but with less initial strength. The obvious sign of excitement is the erection produced by the inflow of blood into the muscular cavities of the penis.

2. Plateau Phase

The excitement process increases until it reaches this phase where it levels off. This phase may last anything from a few minutes up to an hour. Pulse rate, blood pressure and breathing increase in both partners.

2. Plateau Phase

In the male, the penis reaches its maximum size and the glans takes on a more shiny, glowing color due to increased blood circulation and the pressure of the skin. A small secretion of seminal fluid often occurs which contains spermatozoa capable of fertilizing an egg.

3. Orgasmic Phase

The orgasm, the peak of sexual pleasure both in men and in women, is caused by muscular contractions which produce a very intense pleasurable sensation.

3. Orgasmic Phase

In the male, orgasm is brought about by the friction of moving the penis against the vaginal passage walls. When the climax draws near, the sphincter of the urinary bladder closes completely and the muscles at the base of the penis produce contractions which reach the penis, the prostate gland and the seminal vesicles. These contractions push the semen along the urethral passage whilst at the same time producing extreme pleasure lasting around eight to ten seconds. Semen is a substance containing hundreds of millions of spermatozoa and it is essentially composed of protein.

4. Resolution Phase

This consists of a period of physical and psychological relaxation after the climax of the orgasm. The man and woman's sex organs return to their normal size and softness. As in all the preceding phases, the man is faster in the resolution phase. On average for him it will last a couple of minutes, whilst a woman needs 10 to 15 minutes (or longer) to finish this phase.

FEMALE

1. Excitement Phase

In the woman the most exciting messages are those of a tactile nature and she requires a longer period of time to reach excitement than a man does. A woman begins and maintains this phase by hugs, kisses and multiple caresses. The external signs of excitement in a woman are vaginal lubrication in preparation for penetration, although it does not imply that she desires immediate coitus.

2. Plateau Phase

In the woman, the vaginal passage reaches its maximum size in preparation for intercourse and adopts a sack-like shape to house the sperm. Furthermore, in her vulva, around the labia minora, the Bartholin glands secrete a mucus-like substance which will assist in penetration and due to its alkalinity will prolong the life of the spermatozoa up to ten hours in this medium. Her clitoris is at its largest and most sensitive and her nipples become noticeably erect and smooth.

3. Orgasmic Phase

Most women reach orgasm by direct stimulation of the clitoris and a smaller number by friction in the vagina. The female orgasm is associated with contractions of the uterus and adjacent muscles which produce a sensation of immense pleasure not just in the genital area but all over her body.

PRACTICAL IMPLICATIONS

1. Excitement Phase

Due to his visual preferences a man needs to see a woman's naked body and to contemplate its curves. On the other hand, due to her tactile preferences she needs him to caress her.

The sexual differences are marked between men and women and he must recognize that a woman requires more time than a man to reach the point of maximum excitement. It is therefore necessary for a man to learn to slow his impetus down and give more time for her excitement.

2. Plateau Phase

Here also a man tends to need less time than a woman to finish this stage and pass on to the next. It is therefore convenient to prolong this plateau phase, for the enjoyment of both parties. To do so it is important to delay ejaculation. For her part, a woman needs him to caress her clitoris and its cap to keep up her state of enjoyment.

After sufficient games and caresses both are ready for penetration. For this reason, this takes place at the end of the plateau phase.

3. Orgasmic Phase

A simultaneous orgasm is rare and it is unrealistic to propose it as an objective in sex because of the physiological barriers encountered. The vagina has very few nerve endings connected to the parts of the brain concerned with pleasure, whilst the clitoris has many. Furthermore, as the penis does not reach the clitoris during intercourse, we have to conclude that orgasmic synchronicity is somewhat rare. For this reason most sexologists recommend non-simultaneous orgasms.

4. Resolution Phase

This difference between the sexes indicates that a man should not go to sleep or take up other routine activities. During this phase of calmness the couple can talk about the sexual act they have just experienced and the most pleasurable details. It is a time for being together and chatting about nice things, which produces a feeling of exhilaration and fosters mutual closeness and appreciation.

The art of communicating

Communication is undoubtedly **the center of interpersonal relations.** Within the couple, communication is the manner by which messages are exchanged, resulting in satisfaction and happiness or alternatively, causing hurt and resentment.

The process is sufficiently complex to produce variance between the message sent and the message received. Below are some aspects which highlight the complexity of communication:

1. The message is not just what is said

Every spoken message comprises three components:
- The content (the literally spoken word).
- The tone in which it is said (for example the volume, speed or rhythm of voice).
- Non-verbal components (for example facial expression, movements, distance and the behavior itself which accompanies the message).

DIFFERENCES IN SPEAKING

Woman

1. She gives a dramatic account of the facts using varied voice tone, pauses and expression.

2. She speaks more quickly than a man.

3. She prefers to speak about people, relation-ships and the feelings people experience.

4. She is normally dominated by the right hemisphere of the brain: Language, feelings, relationships; the human side of life.

5. She tends to stay on the topic of conversation.

6. She frequently uses plural terms (our house, our children).

7. She quite often reveals her own experiences, emotions and feelings to her husband.

Man

1. He informs of the facts concisely, without going into detail and without resorting to drama.

2. He speaks more slowly than a woman.

3. He prefers to speak about things and events rather than about feelings or people.

4. He tends to be dominated by the left part of the brain: it concerns logic, analysis and competitiveness; the productive side of life.

5. He can easily change the topic of conversation.

6. He tends to use singular terms (my house, my children).

7. He tends toward objective conversation and avoids showing his experiences, emotions and feelings.

Woman	Man
1. She employs plenty of attention indicators: Nodding her head, smiling, saying: "Mm.", "Ah.", "Yes.", "Of course!"	1. He uses attention indicators very sparingly: Nodding his head, smiling, saying: "Mm.", "Ah.", "Yes.", "Of course!"
2. She maintains constant eye contact.	2. He maintains sporadic eye contact.
3. She interprets attention indicators as a sign of interest.	3. He interprets attention indicators as a sign of agreement.
4. She waits for pauses to ask questions.	4. He tends to interrupt to ask questions.
5. She puts any activity aside to listen.	5. He often listens whilst doing something else.

All the studies coincide in their findings regarding the order of importance of these three components in the communication between a couple.

For example: Margaret is serious and sulky (something out of the ordinary for her). When her husband asks her: "What's up?", she replies: "Nothing." The content of her words clearly do not correspond to the facts. Therefore, he must pay attention to the other non-verbal indicators to gather correct information.

2. Every message uses a code

A person sending a message encodes his thoughts. And the person receiving the message has to interpret it using the same code.

When Adrian says to his wife: "Come on little one, don't think any more of it", she might misunderstand the message because she understands the expression "little one" as referring to a child or a teenager and she could think he

is calling her immature. Whilst in the region where Adrian grew up, this expression is used between adults as a term of affection.

3. There are messages with a strong emotional component

The content of a message very rarely reflects emotion. We have to observe non-verbal components to discover such emotions.

When Luisa talks about her parents she is moved and she sometimes sheds a tear. Luisa's parents are very important to her and those tears mean she is proud of them. However, her husband could think that there is a problem or childhood trauma concerning her parents and herself.

4. A message has secondary intentions

With the exception of cliché messages ("Hello, how are you?") most content corresponds to a specific intention. And this is not only true for the sender

but also for the receiver who has to interpret the message.

When Maria arrives home from work, she says to her husband, "What an exhausting day!". This does not mean she is overtired, but rather it is a call for attention so that her husband shows some interest and talks to her. However he, reading other intentions into the message, interprets it differently: "She's telling me that she doesn't want to make love tonight."

5. The interpretation depends on the quality of the relationship

When a relationship is ideal, there are no communication errors, but if a relationship is deteriorating even the sweetest of words will be wrongly interpreted.

Thus, when the relationship is positive there is no problem at all with her saying: *"Raurie, don't be such a perfectionist!"* However, if the relationship is fragile and he arrives with a bouquet of flowers and adulations, she could well wonder: *"And what's this all about? What's he up to now?"*

David Olson and a team of researchers from the University of Minnesota, carried out a study (Olson, D.H., Fye, S. and Olson, A., 1999) in which over 20,000 couples took part. In their findings they identified "happy" couples and those who were considered "unsuited" because of the difficulties they presented. A majority of the happy couples agreed with the following phrases:

- "I am satisfied with the way my husband/wife speaks to me."
- "My husband/wife does not make humiliating comments about me."
- "I have no problem in asking my husband/wife what I want."
- "I find it easy to express my true feelings to my husband/wife."

On the other hand, only 10-12% of the "unsuited" couples agreed with these statements. The conclusion indicates a crystal clear relationship between communication and the success of a couple.

Other similar studies have highlighted that successful couples …

- speak for longer than couples with problems;
- are better listeners and are better at discerning their spouse's feelings and emotions;
- speak not only about their children and their jobs but on a wide range of topics;
- keep their communication channels open, thus facilitating constant dialog;
- Make good use of non-verbal communication.

One of the secrets of good communication is holding conversations at all levels. John Powell (Powel, J., 1974) established five levels of interpersonal communication. When a couple restricts themselves to the most superficial types of communication (levels 1 and 2), their relationship may be in danger. It is therefore necessary to put aside some time to foster communication at the highest possible level.

In the couple, as in other interpersonal relationships, **listening is a difficult task**. People show a marked tendency to concentrate on themselves and not on their partners. Thus, the art of listening should be a learning priority, where practice is necessary before results emerge.

The unit entitled *"Becoming a better listener"*, on page 40, provides useful advice for improving attention and understanding for both partners in a couple.

A good marriage provides the ideal framework for mental healt. We all need to satisfy our need to be accepted, loved and understood. We all need to confide our most intimate secrets, our doubts, our insecurities and our inclinations. This **"unveiling of oneself"** only occurs in the most intimate of circumstances. And it is within the couple that we find the ideal context to satisfy this need.

In a marriage relationship we find someone willing to listen, to understand, to respect our trust and to continue loving us. And when there is a mutual exchange of this kind, friendship and commitment deepen and the relationship prospers. Thus, a married relationship forms an excellent **psychotherapeutic environment** which prevents emotional imbalance.

But when a couple is unable to satisfy this need, one of them (or sometimes both) suffers this deficiency, and so seeks his or her satisfaction outside of marriage: For example a wife entrusts a friend with her feelings and it is this friend to whom she unveils herself. Or a husband feels captivated by another woman who appears to listen with more interest than does his own wife. When this deficiency lasts for a long time within a marriage, it brings about a crisis and ends in separation.

Therefore, it is fundamental that every couple strives to keep this area of their relationship healthy and thus avoid the consequent marital crisis.

Any careful assessment of conversations will highlight **differences between men and women**. Without even listening to what they say, women are seen to use more non-verbal communication than men. Women laugh more, move more, and use more facial gestures and sounds (ah!, mm!) than men.

This is not only true when they speak but also when they listen. Within the couple, ignoring such differences will induce a man to interpret the communication process using his own patterns and a woman using hers. And this may provoke conflict. The boxes on pages 36 and 37 give an overview of the typical differences between men and women as far as speaking and listening are concerned.

Men and women tend to judge their interlocutor following their own particular communication styles. For example:

- If a woman does not receive clear attention indicators when she is talking to her husband about something important, she will assume that he is not paying attention.

- If a man receives those indicators from his wife, he will assume that she completely agrees with him.

Becoming a better listener

1. **Use of attention indicators**. It is not only necessary to pay attention but also to show you are paying attention.

   Nod or shake your head; look a person in the eye; say, "yes", "mm", "of course", "I see"; adopt a posture which indicates attention and interest.

2. **Caution in showing one's position**. Good communication precludes competition between "my" position and "your" position. Within a couple communication should be about learning more about each other's feelings and not about winning or losing.

   When a wife is trying to express to her husband that he does not devote time to the children, it would be a mistake for him to immediately say: "But last Sunday I took them to see a football match." Although this may be true, it does not help to soothe his wife's feelings and could even result in a confrontation.

3. **Interpreting non-verbal messages**. As we have already said, a couple verbal communication constitutes only a minimal part of all their communication.

   Marianne bought a new summer dress. "Well, how do you like this dress?" "Yes it's very pretty," replied Louis, "but we've got to be packing." The following day they had a huge fight over something trivial. After a long talk, the real reason came out. Louis had not known how to read Marianne's message that she wanted more of his attention.

4. **Assuring proper understanding of message**. One of the very most effective ways of doing this is to paraphrase certain key parts of the message to confirm that it is being understood.

   David confides in his wife an incident that has happened to him at work. After asking him to write a report, his superior invites him in, looks at the file disdainfully and says, "Why so many pages? You could have explained this on one sheet!" "So," David adds, "I'm feeling low, tired, furious and want to leave this job." His wife rightly comments., "I see the incident has got to you, left you worn out and now you want to give it all up. Tell me more about what happened."

5. **Respecting the interlocutor**. A crass mistake on the part of a listener is to immediately forward his or her opinion or offer a piece of advice.

   In the previous example, David's wife would have taken the wrong route had she said, "Don't even think about resigning from your job. Before leaving a permanent post you have to think it through and above all, you have to have another job to go to …" With this message she would have turned the conversation into a heated discussion over whether he should leave his job or not. But David does not actually want to leave his job. What he needs is to get over his disappointment with the help of his wife's attention and understanding.

6. **Caution in replies**. The retort is a typical conversational tactic when a discussion or verbal fight is in progress. It consists of concentrating on preparing a reply as opposed to listening.

   Martin's wife complains to him that every time she cleans the washbasin it is full of stubble from his morning shave. Instead of listening, Martin is thinking of the times he, himself, has cleaned the washbasin after using it and is preparing his own rejoinder reminding her of when she moves his tools around.

7. **Use imagery**. Personal worries can easily dominate listeners' minds and distract them for a moment. One of the most useful method of avoiding this mental flight is to sketch the situation being described in your mind's eye.

   When a wife tells her husband of a problem she is experiencing with a colleague at work, he imagines the situation she is referring to: His wife, her colleague, her boss, everyone in the middle of the office having a lively conversation, papers in hand etc. This visual image keeps the husband's attention and enhances his understanding of the problem.

What in time tends to become a simple and peaceful routine is usually one of the points of conflict in the early years of married life. This is partly due to lack of habit for the newlyweds and partly because resources tend to be limited.

It is therefore necessary to begin married life employing **good financial administration** of the couple's resources. Perhaps the most efficient way is to draw up a budget that controls the family economy on a weekly or monthly basis.

Making up a budget can be a waste of time unless certain basic principles are adhered to. Here are the most important of these principles:

The budget ...

• **... must be a joint project**. The figures have to reflect mutual agreement between man and wife.

• **... has to include a section for fixed costs**. Fixed costs (food, rent or mortgage payments, bills etc.) are untouchable and funds assigned to them must never be used for other purposes.

• **... must have an underpinning aim or philosophy to guide it**. If work is an important aspect, then expenditure related to work (training courses, tools, equipment ...) will have priority, and if housing is important, so will its corresponding expenditure (mortgage, repairs ...). After these preferential items will come other secondary items which can be reduced if necessary.

ALARM SIGNALS IN FAMILY SPENDING

There are people who, in spite of enjoying a good income, find themselves in a critical position because they use and abuse their lines of credit (cards, hire-purchase plans, loans etc.). Below we have outlined some warning indicators. If the reader answers any the following points affirmatively he or she should be on their guard.

You create risks when ...

1. You pay 15% or more of your net income in paying off debts (excluding the mortgage on your home).

2. You use credit to acquire goods which could be bought interest-free within the next few months.

3. You have to use credit to acquire essential goods (for example your weekly household shopping).

4. You borrow to pay off old debt.

5. You have to think which of your creditors you will pay first.

6. At a given moment you find it difficult to calculate how much you owe.

7. You need to borrow money from family, friends and neighbors.

8. Loss of employment would immediately bankrupt you.

- **... must be made bearing exceptional costs in mind.** There are costs which come up once or twice a year. To cater for these it is necessary to regularly put some money aside on a monthly basis.

- **... must include a sum for unforeseen expenditure every month.**

- **... must be followed wherever possible**. If we are constantly making exceptions we render our budget worthless. Nevertheless, it should incorporate a certain amount of flexibility.

A **realistic budget** will prevent excessive spending on trimmings which can be put off for times when funds are more plentiful.

It is vital to highlight the risk associated with the use of loans and lines of credit. The repayments carry interest charges, and those who use them find their buying power is immediately reduced. In other words, using **loans and credit** leads to impoverishment.

There are cases where use of credit is more than justified. For example buying a home is a wise investment in which, while interest is charged, the benefits (tax relief, investment revaluation) compensate the expense. The purchase of a vehicle on credit is also justified, especially if it is used for work, as is credit to set up a business.

However, there are people who always use credit when they do not have cash in hand. Be aware of the alarm signals, like those listed on the sidebar.

And beware of credit and debit cards. Their use has to be controlled if we do not want to find ourselves with an unpleasant surprise at the end of the month.

The type of relationship a couple has is linked to the concept they have of themselves.

John Crosby proposed three basic types of relationship (Crosby, J.E. 1979):

The dependent relationship

The joint identity of the couple is over-pronounced. The partners have a relationship in which the absence of one renders the other almost useless. The "I" of one is fused into that of the other. Crosby represents this relationship with a capital **A**.

- The dependent relationship implies poor self-esteem in one, or sometimes both partners in a couple, which may lead to significant dysfunctions.

The interdependent relationship

The joint identity is balanced. The partners in the couple influence and support each other and enjoy a satisfactory life together whilst each one maintains their own "I". The absence of one affects the other but they can survive alone. This is represented by a capital **M**.

- In the interdepent relationship both partners possess a healthy level of self-esteem which gives rise to a rewarding relationship.

The independent relationship

There is no joint identity. Each partner is self-supporting and does not need the other. The absence of one has no effect on the other. This is symbolized by a capital **H**.

- Lastly, in the independent relationship the partners, with or without self-esteem maintain a superficial relationship where their achievements and failures are individual and not shared in the couple. As a result, their life together does not fulfill its aim.

To achieve an interdependent relationship it is necessary to nurture each other's self-esteem.

The dependent relationship

The interdependent relatioship

The independent relationship

When children arrive

Chapter Summary

*T*he alarm clock goes off. Gareth gets ready for work while Iona prepares everything before awaking their daughters (aged 8 and 4). They eat a hasty breakfast and leave home soon after. The school bus picks the girls up.

Iona only works mornings, therefore when she leaves work she can pick her younger daughter up from kindergarten. Once home, they have lunch and she puts the child to bed for a nap. In the meantime she does the housework and later takes her to the park. Gareth finishes in time to pick up their elder daughter. When he gets home he plays with the children while Iona does the ironing and supervises homework. After helping Iona in the kitchen, they have supper and Iona puts the girls to bed while Gareth washes the dishes. They are both tired.

This couple have realized that they never have time to talk calmly nor to be alone together even for a short while … Therefore, they have decided to put one weekend aside per month to go away together, just the two of them (the girls stay with their grandparents). It costs them financially, but they have come to the conclusion that an unhappy marriage would be a much more expensive and painful experience.

Given the complexity of being parents and the need to maintain the quality of a marriage, these family years require careful planning. Although it is not possible to guarantee total happiness, we can say that, with due **preparation and planning**, the crises which arise may be turned into manageable difficulties.

Irresponsible parenthood proves extremely costly for parents, children and society in general. Many mistakes made by young people who are unfit for parenthood carry a very high price. For this reason it is wise to familiarize oneself with these aspects and take the simple step of **preventing** pregnancy.

A husband and wife who wishto become parents must ...

1. **Be mentally and physically prepared**. A positive attitude is fundamental during the prenatal period, especially for the mother, although the father may play a decisive role in his wife's state of mind through his behavior and attitude. As far as physical preparation is concerned, a fetus is at risk if its mother is undernourished, takes certain medicines or consumes alcohol, tobacco, caffeine, marihuana or other narcotics. If the mother is a carrier of the AIDS virus there is also a strong likelihood that this will be passed on to the fetus. A further risk is also involved if the mother contracts certain illnesses; German measles, diabetes, tuberculosis, syphilis … The father is not exempt from responsibility. The use of marihuana, tobacco, alcohol and other drugs produces defective spermatozoa (see Lester, R. and Van Theil, D.H., 1977).

2. **Wait until they are in a sound economic and material situation**. Having a child demands a minimum of quality in terms of lifestyle, with enough stable income to take on the regular costs incurred by a newborn child and during the years thereafter. This includes providing a general environment which is favorable for their children's psychological and physical development (Fraga, C.G., et al, 1991).

3. **Wait until they are in a sound emotional situation**. Newlywed or very young couples need time for their relationship to mature and to adapt to married life. In this way both will be better prepared to take on the responsibility of parenthood.

4. **Have all aspects of their legal and social expectations in order**. It is essential to consider the social and legal implications of having children outside of a formalized relationship. For however much a society may tolerate or admit special circumstances, parents must think of the problems that the aforesaid situations engender and act responsibly.

5. **Be prepared to make sacrifices**. Being parents brings enormous satisfaction. The majority of parents would not change it for anything in the world. However, being good parents implies personal endeavor and sacrifice. It requires time, money, physical and emotional energy and changes to timetables and habits.

6. **Respect their children**. They cannot be thought of as property. They should never be physically, psychologically or sexually exploited. As they grow up they begin to voice their own opinions, which their parents have the right to try to

45

sway. However, if this does not happen they must accept and respect these differences of opinion.

7. **Pass values and ideals on to their children in order to guide them for the rest of their lives**. Parents have the moral obligation to prepare their children to be useful men and women, bearing principles and values which are not only advantageous to them but to society as a whole. They should also transmit their ideas and moral and religious traditions by way of advice and above all by setting a good example. Sometimes, when children come of age and become independent, their way of thinking and acting may be in opposition to their parents' ideals. In these circumstances parents should warn, advise, negotiate … but if no consensus can be reached, they will have to let their children take their own road and live the consequences; this is a sad road to take, but one which has to be contemplated as a possibility in the role of a parent.

Special decisions

In contrast to the traditional tendency of getting married and immediately having children, couples today make plans to become parents at the most suitable moment. Others consider adoption and opt for this route. Others prefer not to experience parenthood.

To postpone

It is becoming increasingly more common to wait a few years before having offspring.

There are valid reasons for this: To finish studying, to launch a professional career which initially requires exclusive dedication, or to consolidate a marital relationship in order to bring children into the world at a more favorable moment. According to research findings, the quality of parenthood among couples who have postponed having children is better than that of very young parents, and the satisfaction derived from the arrival of a baby is also greater. However, postponing for too long engenders the risk of not being able to conceive, complications in gestation and pregnancy, and the difficulties associated with bringing up young children at an advanced age.

To adopt

The secret system of adoption by which nobody knew the process and suddenly a newborn child appeared in the family, is one which belongs to the past. In smaller communities this resulted in everyone knowing that the child was adopted except the child itself who would find out sooner or later. Today the process is much more transparent and is becoming popular among those people who cannot have children, as

well as amongst those who already have children. The experience can be highly rewarding, both for the former and the latter. Crossing the bridge of adoption usually indicates a high degree of altruism, which favors love between the child and its adopted parents, as well as the satisfaction of having helped an infant whose natural parents could not take on the responsibility of its care.

Not to have

Although a minority, there are some couples who decide not to have children. Their friends and family usually react to this saying that they are selfish, that it is not possible to be truly in love and not have children, that they would not have been born if their parents had felt the same or that they will be unhappy if they remain childless. It is not good to criticize such positions. Some people take such decisions for professional reasons or because they want greater freedom; others think that they are not cut out to be parents; others look at life and its risks and conclude that it is not worth bringing children into such a world. The decision should be respected, especially when it is the will of both spouses after having weighed the advantages and disadvantages.

Sometimes it is necessary to postpone having a family until a more favorable moment in the future. This is an extremely important topic, even when a couple already has children and does not wish to further increase the family because of the destabilization effect it might have. The box on the following page offers a variety of valid options for planning conception in a responsible way.

In order to decide on a contraception method, the couple's **personal circumstances** must be considered, sufficient **professional guidance** should be received, the **alternatives** should be discussed and a joint decision taken. Family planning is a matter for both spouses and it is inappropriate to lay all the responsibility on only one partner.

When the couple are young, it is unadvisable to opt for **sterilization** of either partner, even though they may already have children. The family circumstances may change in the future and this method is, to all intents and purposes, irreversible. Neither is the **IUD** recommended for couples who decide not to have children for the time being but wish to at a later date; due to the risk of the woman becoming sterile.

A crucial question that a couple must ask themselves is: How much of an upset would an **unwanted pregnancy** cause? If a couple, for whatever reason, cannot or should not have children, it is necessary for them to consider methods with a low failure rate, such as contraceptive pills or hormone implants. At the same time, it is necessary to bear in mind that these methods produce significant side effects in certain women, and health complications should be avoided. Before starting a course of oral contraception it is necessary to undergo a medical examination and to follow the advice of a gynecologist.

If the couple does not want to have children for the moment, but if in the event of pregnancy, the upset would be minor, then barrier methods are more recommendable, especially the condom as it is highly reliable without any side effects.

Women with regular periods can take advantage of a combination of natural methods. Taken together they provide a good indication of the moment of ovulation. This method requires that by mutual agreement they decline intercourse on certain days of the month. However, the procedure, if well managed, is harmless, cheap, with no side effects and relatively effective.

CONTRACEPTIVE METHODS

Method	Description	Efficiency
Sterilization	Surgical intervention which consists of a ligature in the woman's Fallopian tubes or the sectioning of the deferens passage in the man (a procedure known as vasectomy). The method is permanent or very difficult to reverse.	>99%
Contraceptive Pill	Pills taken orally which contain a certain combination of hormones to avoid fertilization. They help to regulate the menstrual cycle, prevent ovarian cysts and inflammation of the pelvis. However, they may cause vomiting, obesity, aching breasts, fatigue and a decrease in sexual appetite amongst other symptoms.	97%
Condom	An elongated covering of very fine, resistant rubber which is placed over the male sex organ before penetration to avoid semen being introduced into the vaginal passage. The method may fail if it is not used from the beginning of intercourse, if it is not in good condition or if it breaks.	88%
Diaphragm	A small, very fine rubber cap surrounded by a metal ring which is placed by the woman in the upper part of the vaginal passage to avoid semen entering the womb. It may fail due to incorrect positioning, if it is withdrawn in the eight hours following intercourse, if it is broken or if insufficient spermicide is used. It sometimes produces allergies or localized infection.	82%
Cervical cap	A small rubber or plastic cap in the shape of a thimble which a doctor places in the highest part of the vaginal passage. It works in exactly the same way as the diaphragm but can be left in place for long periods. It should also be used in conjunction with a spermicidal cream.	82%
Intrauterine Device	A plastic object, available in various shapes which is placed inside the womb by a doctor through the vaginal passage. This object produces an inflammatory reaction in the uterus which attracts white blood corpuscles. These, in turn, produce substances which are poisonous for the spermatozoa impeding the fertilization of the egg. This method can cause serious localized infections, excessive menstruation as well as permanent sterility in the woman..	98%
Spermicides	These are creams or foams which the woman inserts in her vagina with an applicator prior to intercourse. These substances eliminate the spermatozoa, thus avoiding fertilization. They may fail if applied too early or in insufficient quantities. They may produce allergic reactions.	79%
Hormonal implants	A doctor inserts a tiny device under the skin on the woman's arm. The device secretes the hormone progesterone in sufficient quantities to prevent fertilization. It is effective for five years. The side effects are the same as those for the contraceptive pill.	>99%
Natural methods	This consists of planning intercourse for those days in the month when fertilization is unlikely. To achieve this the woman uses various indicators: An exact knowledge of her cycle calendar; the variations in her body temperature; and the changes in the quantity and consistency of her cervical mucus. In this way she can estimate the approximate day of ovulation to thus avoid intercourse on the days immediately before and after this day	80-90%

The arrival of the first child is a transcendental landmark in a couple's life. Although enough months pass from the moment the pregnancy is detected through to birth for them to get used to the idea of becoming parents and to prepare themselves for this event, a baby's arrival, especially that of the first-born, makes a great impression.

This is how the author of this book remembers the moments after his wife Annette's first delivery:

"When I saw my newborn little girl, dirty and covered in blood, I didn't feel the least bit tender. Even less when they put a tube into her mouth to suck the remains of blood and other fluids from her stomach. But then I was able to perceive Claudia's resourcefulness: Whilst the nurse was inserting the tube, my five-minute-old baby girl had grabbed the tube and pulled at it with both hands to free herself of what was bo-thering her.

One hour later, when Annette was sleeping, worn out by the delivery, they brought our baby girl in, clean, dressed and sleeping in a crib. It was then that I felt the tenderness which hadn't come initially. 'These are the delights of being a father. What a delectable and peaceful little face!' I thought, 'we're all tired; it's time to sleep."

An hour later, Claudia began to make a noise as if she were gently gargling. She seemed to be sleeping peacefully but she was still making that noise. Looking at her relaxed face I felt embarrassed to call the nurse to ask if that was normal …

I lay down and tried to go back to sleep, but I couldn't. The "gargling" lasted on and off for three or four hours. Lying on that hospital sofa, I didn't get a moment's sleep all night. Lying there I wondered: 'Will every night be like this? What is it to be a father?'"

Indeed, with all the fuss of the birth and everything around it, the parents do not realize the real effect the new arrival has on the family. Weeks later, an analysis of their daily activities will show that the couple's life has changed completely.

The presence of children is capable of strengthening a marital relationship and providing the couple with a further source of happiness. Both feel more united through the presence of their first child, born precisely out of their love for each other. The baby's care and its daily progress are a source of satisfaction to its parents.

With the joy … can come problems

It is true that the arrival of children is one of great joy, but we cannot ignore that this event can interfere in a couple's relationship and distance them, a fact for which they should be prepared. Family dynamics undoubtedly change completely. Nevertheless, by employing certain preventive measures we can turn these years into memorable ones, full of satisfaction.

what is lost in each scenario. Once an agreement has been made, the prospects for success are very high, regardless of the chosen option.

When a wife hears a calling to devote herself exclusively to her wifely and motherly duties, this is the ideal situation. The role of mother and teacher provides many advantages, as long as she feels satisfied and realized in these duties. However women's participation in the workforce is unmistakable as is their capacity to carry out tasks traditionally assigned to men. Therefore, dialog and agreements that satisfy both spouses become essential but, at the same time, should not undermine their children's needs.

- **Another factor impinging on the success of a family with children is the quality of the marital relationship.** For a couple who enjoy a loving and co-operative relation-ship, the arrival of children does not provoke crises nor traumas. The best gift a father can give to his children is said to be that of loving their mother. A loving, attentive, considerate and willing husband will drive away any feeling of dissatisfaction his wife may have. A wife displaying the same characteristics will complete the circle.

Let us consider some of the factors which may exert a negative influence on these delightful years:

- **The parents' expectations are often mistaken.** Perhaps because parenthood has often been described as a romantic and idealized experience, the work and sacrifice it requires has not been underlined. For this reason, future parents should not expect everything to be idyllic, but rather they should understand that the experience has different perspectives, some enjoyable, others not so. Young parents (around twenty years of age) or those, who have not made plans for parenthood together find this new situation more of a strain. However, older couples or those who have carefully planned the moment for having a family are less affected.

- **Both spouses working outside the home is a factor which may worsen the stress during those early years.** This system has its advantages and disadvantages. Therefore, a consensus decision should be reached, assessing what is gained and

A year after its birth when a child begins to walk and explore its environment, the task of supervision becomes more tiring. The following years up to the age of kindergarten are hard. Many couples discover that having children is more difficult than they had expected. Mothers, who are usually in charge of their children's upbringing, complain that fathers do not help out enough. All of these things may be a prelude to a marriage crisis. Nevertheless, this may be avoided, and to do so it is important to count on survival strategies. Try the following:

Filter everything through the crystal of a good sense of humor

To overcome this difficult stage you have to see the funny side of things. After all is said and done, once this stage is over, no one looks back on it with bitterness. Laughing is preferable to crying.

Carry out "group therapy" with other parents

There is no more useful activity for keeping yourself sane than joining up with other fathers and mothers, while the children are playing in the park or at home, to exchange experiences concerning children. Not only is it pedagogical (a lot can be learned in the aforesaid meetings) but it is also therapeutic, as you leave the meetings with a feeling of relief when you confirm that others experience the same problems as you do.

Nurture your relationship with your partner

The marital relationship is basic and fundamental as a support system. When the spouses enjoy optimal relationship, the physical and emotional demands placed on them by their children are reduced. This is why it is important to devote time and care to making your spouse happy. Regularly put aside a time to get away together, either with the help of a relative or a babysitter.

Seek support from the family

Be it from one side or the other, grandparents, aunts and uncles … are usually willing to lend a hand. Mothers and daughters tend to feel closer than ever at this time. In reasonable doses, this family support can prove of great benefit to all parties.

Be very patient

Changes in children and their maturing process take time, but it does happen. It helps to think of each stage as unique and unrepeatable in order to make the most of each one.

A reorganization of duties

Men seem to suffer an inner apprehension of losing control of their home and their role as head of the family. Because their profession, their job constitutes their main source of self-esteem, they are also afraid of losing what feeds their ego.

Women, by allowing men to do tasks traditionally set aside for them, may feel hounded in their heart of hearts. They feel they are losing ground, that they are being invaded in their own territory.

It is true that many men give a very poor performance as far as housework is concerned. Perhaps because they were never allowed to learn. The fact is, that not knowing how to do a job well, they shrink away from it.

These obstacles can be overcome by **frank conversation** between spouses.

Putting aside reproaches, the couple should speak and listen to each other in order to find solutions to these problems which are valid for both parties: Why do I not collaborate more? What can I do well? What can I learn to do? Do my children need me? Simply talking these topics through will help both to feel better and to vary the assignment of tasks when necessary.

One practical aspect which will undoubtedly serve to resolve many differences, is the ability of spouses to talk, to negotiate and to reach agreements concerning their respective duties in the home, their children's upbringing and any other topics which may arise. The box below on this page presents a step-by-step plan for negotiation and page 54 contains advice to foster better communication.

TO NEGOTIATE

Betty Carter, founder and manager of the Westchester Family Institute, recommends a simple and effective method for spouses to reach agreements which are satisfactory to both parties. This plan is designed especially for couples with children at home. According to Carter, the preliminary task is to understand that a marital relationship is egalitarian. If this is clear, the negotiation process is easy. It is necessary to:

1. Know what you want.
2. Express it clearly and calmly.
3. Listen to your spouse's position and try to understand it completely.
4. Make your way towards a win-win solution by which neither party loses; for example, both sides make concessions at the same time or alternately.
5. If negotiation fails, present a viable alternative.

Dialog proves to be fundamental

With the family bustle of a home with children, partners may become tired and frustrated at the never-ending list of duties. At this time, they may say hurtful things which are difficult to wipe out. They are usually about topics which are:

- Delicate.
- Of contrasting opinions.
- Liable to hurt the other.
- Concerning the need for a change of habit in the other.

In these cases we have to be careful to talk without putting the blame for the problem on the other (at least all of the blame). The solution is to use "I-messages". Use expressions (usually in first person) which reveal our feelings, leaving a spouse room for change.

The box below on this page provides some illustrations of this type of message.

Learning to establish simple, smooth dialogs, without anger, without blaming, without victimizing, and with each partner making the best contribution he or she can enhance the well-being of any stage of a marriage, but fundamentally in stages involving change.

I-MESSAGES

Isabel and Peter are parents of two children below school-age. His job involves quite a lot of traveling and she does substitute teaching at an elementary school from time to time. In order to enjoy some privacy on a regular basis they decided to have supper together in the evenings when Peter was not away. She prepares the supper every day with great care in order to enjoy that special moment in the day with her husband. However, he is unpredictable.

Sometimes he arrives in time for supper, other times he is late, often by up to two or three hours. This deeply annoys Isabel and she decides the best thing to do is talk this through with him so that he can organize himself to get home in time or, alternatively, to warn her so that she can change the time supper is served.

- **Option n^{er} 1. An ineffective and belligerent message.** "Peter! Look at the time! You are inconsiderate, selfish … (more and more upset). Here I am, making sacrifices, fighting with the kids, slaving away to cook your favorite dishes … and you stroll in fresh as a daisy … as if this were a restaurant. For you I'm just a servant, but you're mistaken. I'm not going to put up with this any longer. Either you get here on time, or …"

- **Option n^{er} 2. An I-message which does not blame, and is likely to be effective.** "Peter, I expect you have a reason for being late, but this is a very important time of the day for me and I think it is for you too. When you don't come home I get worried, I feel hurt and

sometimes I even think that your friends or your job are more important to you than I am … though I know it isn't like that … What can be done so that you can get home on time? And if any time you can't make it, I'd like you to call so that we can at least make a change of plans".

Notice that the phrases in the first option are in the second person in the main (you are, you think), whereas those in the second option are in the first person (I get worried, I feel hurt, I know that …).

Speaking about the weather, the news, work or the children is not serious when there are no problems. But there are particular topics and circumstances for each couple in which they have to temper their words and gestures. The following advice may be useful in these situations:

1 *Do not speak until your partner has finished.* Try to listen with the utmost attention.

2 *Think about what you are going to say.* Think before you speak, especially if you are upset. If in doubt do not speak.

3 *Do not speak reproachfully.* Words spoken in a reprimanding tone do not bring about the desired effect, even if they are full of wisdom.

4 *Focus on the positive side.* Although the topic is a thorny one, take a break and stop to say something positive.

5 *Speak slowly and without shouting.* A slow, gentle voice in conversation is conducive to calmness and tranquility.

6 *Tell the truth.* It is not good to tell lies, even white lies. Being truthful brings its rewards, but you have to do so with love and tact.

7 *Avoid confrontations.* You and your spouse do not have to agree on every-thing. There will always be some areas of disagreement. But this does not mean that they must end in a fight.

8 *Openly admit it when you are to blame.* This will cause a positive reaction in your partner.

9 *Avoid anger at all costs.* This attitude immediately ruptures the communication process and attention is directed to the state of anger r as opposed to the message.

10 *Speak at the appropriate time.* There are certain moments which are more suited to talking about delicate matters.

"Let them overcome the habits of hasty speech and the desire to blame others ... What harm is wrought in the family circle by the utterance of impatient words, for the impatient utterance of one leads another to retort in the same spirit and manner."

Ellen G. White (1827-1915)

Little by little, as the children enter school age, **family dynamics change**. Now the children spend most of their day at school and family interaction is confined to week-ends and a few hours on work days. Furthermore, the greater part of the children's time with their parents is devoted to some obligation: School homework, shopping or housework duties.

Therefore, the parents' role enters a stage defined by family psychologists as **co-regulation**. The constant control of infancy dissipates with the autonomy of movement attained by school age children who take charge of their own personal care and other duties. In this way, parents continue helping their children in a variety of activities, not by doing things for them but rather supervising how their children do them.

The final objective is **self-regulation** which is reached at the end of the adolescent stage.

Now they look after their own personal hygiene and belongings. When they reach adolescence they can stay at home alone while their parents go out on an errand. They are also able to (and should) help out with household duties and responsibilities according to their age and level of maturity. This situation provides parents with somewhat more independence.

INFANCY

Parental control

SCHOOL-AGE

Co-regulation

ADOLESCENCE

Self-regulation

Families are in a constant state of development from when children are born until the time they leave the home. Over these years couples experience many situations which are a source of satisfaction and sometimes stress.

When children reach adolescence, family dynamics change yet again. The multiple physical and emotional changes of adolescent boys and girls significantly affect family dynamics. It is now necessary to **renegotiate the relationship between parents and children** as well as within the couple. Here are some suggestions for maintaining a balanced family when children reach adolescence:

• **Change technique**. Adolescents reach a level of self-sufficiency whereby they require less help in their studies and with their du-ties and fewer "sermons". Many parents are not ready for this and continue treating their children as if they were still small; this does not usually work.

• **Accept the psychological changes in an adolescent**. Children at this age tend to have a defiant attitude. As long as this does not get out of hand, parents should understand that this constitutes part of their psychological development and they should not overreact to this behavior.

• **Apply caution in certain areas of hazardous behavior**. Adolescence is accompa-nied by certain risks which young people should be warned about: Violent or high risk sports, drugs, sex, antisocial behavior, and so on.

• **Be prepared for emotional changes**. In adolescence it is possible that children feel less close to their parents, insecure, embarrassed when with relatives, nervous with bruised self-esteem … This emotional turmoil should be seen as a passing phase and parents need to exercise patience and treat their children with friendliness as opposed to bad-temperedness.

• **Be prepared to observe problems between siblings**. Adolescents frequently behave belligerently towards their older or younger brothers and sisters. It is good to know that this tends to disappear, or at least to ease, towards the end of this stage as the adolescent feels more sure of him or herself.

• **Understand the role of friends and companions**. Friends and companions exert a strong influence on an adolescent. Parents should not be surprised when their children regard their friends' opinions as almost sacred. This will also wane as they become more mature.

- **Allow adult help from outside the home**. Adolescents usually display a negative attitude toward parental advice. An uncle's advice or that of a teacher or a family friend may be more influential than that of their parents'.

- **Let them participate in family decisions**. Adolescents should take part in drawing up rules and making decisions which affect the family circle, although the moment has not yet arrived for the adolescent's decision to prevail; ra-ther their parents should have the last word.

- **Agree on ques-tions of discipline**. When parents are not in agreement on criteria concerning rules and discipline, the family relationship may be impaired. It may sometimes be the case that an adolescent pleases one parent and displeases the other. This is very unfavorable both for the adolescent and for the spouses' relationship.

- **Stick together in a vital relationship**. The adolescent stage is accompanied by sufficient stress to cause negative effects on parents. How-ever, if these support each other, loving and consoling each other in the difficult times their children may pro-voke, they will more quickly and efficiently find solutions to their problems.

Adolescence is not a problem

Perhaps the title is surprising. It is true that some adolescents are rebellious, un-stable and difficult. But the fact that problems arise during this stage does not convert adolescence into a problem. The birth of a baby also gives rise to difficulties, but it is a natural, normal, common event. Adolescence is some-thing similar.

The most promising stage

We, both parents and educators, have to get used to observing adolescence from a perspective of normality. Some psychologists equate this stage of life to a second birth, which like the first requires preparation.

The trees impede us from seeing the wood. And this is a pity because this wood is the golden age of life. It is the moment of great ideals. This is what provokes great conflict between parents and adolescents who see them with all their defects, unlike during infancy.

It is a stage charged with dreams and hopes. The adolescent is making a final effort to become a member of the adult world. A leap from cocoon to butterfly, which often proves to be painful, like a birth, but also full of promise.

An adolescent needs to be understood and loved more than ever. Although he makes mistakes he has to feel that his parents are with him above all else.

Perhaps if we look back to our own adolescence when in doubt about how to face a difficult situation, we may find a suitable answer.

All parents spend a great amount of time, money and personal effort in meeting the physical needs of their offspring. However, not all of them stop to consider their obligation of passing on values which equip their children to live in society and serve others. Less still do they plan the teaching of these ethical and spiritual principles which underpin this.

One of the most serious threats to this generation is the prevailing idea that passing on values, especially religious values, limits a child's freedom of choice. Thus, it is concluded that it is better not to teach anything and wait until they are old enough to choose their own beliefs. This approach is very dangerous as we are actively educating our children as agnostics. The **family** not only provides the **best context** for education in these principles but constitutes an ideal scenario to exemplify the aforementioned values in an authentic way.

We therefore propose that parents should be instrumental in passing on their beliefs instead of leaving it to the social environment.

Below we have laid out some guidelines for carrying out this transcendental duty:

- **Identify the concrete values which have to be taught**. Every culture and family values to a greater or lesser degree certain attitudes and conduct. Parents should be aware of the ethical, social, moral and religious qualities they wish to give to their children; the following list serves as an example:

  ✓ *Social values:* Respect for others, altruism, courtesy, politeness, cleanliness, tidiness.

  ✓ *Moral values:* Truth, generosity, fairness, self-control, honesty, charity, goodness.

  ✓ *Religious values:* Beliefs, love for God, faith, hope, meditation of the Scriptures, prayer, individual and collective worship.

- **Teach by example**. The teaching of values has to be done using appropriate and correct instructions, explanations, reasoning and illustrations. Furthermore, these said values have to be demonstrated in a practical way through parental

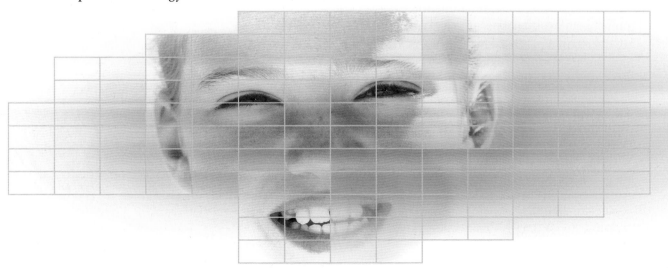

behavior. The compulsory teaching of conducts such as honor or mutual respect would lack all meaning if the parents do not subscribe to them.

- **Take advantage of real life examples**. News, events of one's neighborhood or examples from nature provide an excellent opportunity to introduce and illustrate the human condition, social values or God as our creator. Small children, especially, benefit from these objective lessons and their assimilation results in a solid and stable character.

- **Carry out a humanitarian project as a family**. The teaching of values is definitively strengthened by practice. Thus, if a family proposes to systematically help certain needy people or to take active part in an ecology project for the benefit of the neighborhood as a whole, it is not only teaching but also practicing these values which become instilled in each and every one of the family members.

- **Use the family as a platform for teaching religion**. When parents hold religious beliefs, the family is the principal means of transmiting these on among them. There-fore, family prayer or group reflection of sacred and holy texts or perceiving daily happenings through God's word become everyday activities for their children. In this way they not only develop know-ledge but also how to apply these principles which will make them better people to live with.

According to surveys carried out among couples with children, sexual activity diminishes during this stage compared to the period before children. It is a fact that the professional activities of one, or sometimes both parents added to the time devoted to the care and attention required by children mean that many aspects of married life are affected, one of which is the sex life.

Nevertheless, this does not mean that sex has to decrease in quality. Careful planning can lead to an active and satisfactory sex life during this stage.

Below we have made a series of suggestions to help improve this:

- **Use a good method of contraception**. One's sexuality during this stage is under enough pressure without adding the anxiety of an unwanted pregnancy. Therefore, if the family is complete, sex should be free of such fears by employing the most appropriate contraceptive method. Sexual encounters will then be more relaxed, more complete and will prove highly satisfying.

- **Do not become obsessed by sex**. Social pressure may make many people think that sex is the most important factor in a relationship and when it occurs less frequently, they feel frustrated. But quality is more important than quantity. Sexuality is more than a physical need; it includes emotional rapport, love, identity and mutual affirmation. Sex is a highly important aspect, but not the most important.

- **Aim to attain an optimal relationship**. Good moments in sex do not occur in isolation; they are the result of a satisfactory interpersonal relationship. Displays of love, affection, tenderness and mutual interest are the true pillars for making a sexual encounter something memorable. When there is resentment, suspicion or indifference in a couple's relationship, sex loses all incentive.

- **Nurture self-esteem**. Healthy feelings about oneself are prerequisite to a satisfactory sex life. The wife, especially, needs to feel good about herself to reap enjoyment in any sexual encounter. It is very common that due to her role as the mother of small children and as weight increases, she may feel less sexually attractive. Here she needs her husband's support and his words of praise and approval to build up her self-esteem and predispose her to better sexual relations.

- **Remember the sexual needs of both partners**. A man's sexual satisfaction is not attained by the same means as a woman's and vice-versa. For this reason men should be aware of the needs of their wives, who in turn should be aware of their husbands' needs.

- **Avoid overworking**. Both men and women, when too involved in their work, may experience a syndrome known as **hypoactive or inhibited sexual desire** (see the box on page 89). The solution to this problem consists, in most cases, of reorganizing their lives in such a way as to have time to work, but also to enjoy their families, their spouses and their sexual relations.

- **Revive romantic activities**. Although for a man this may be less interesting, it proves essential for a woman. Most women need romanticism before they can display passion. Thus, we recommend expressions of affection, greeting cards, surprise gifts, love-letters … as well as certain activities which foster romanticism: Organize a special dinner in a restaurant, watch a movie, go away for the weekend or simply go to bed earlier to share an easy conversation before making love.

5 After the children leave home

Chapter Summary

Andrea has just had her fifty-fifth birthday and speaks about her sex life with ease and satisfaction: "My sex life with my husband is better than it has been for years ... perhaps because we know each other better, or because we know each other's needs and tastes. The truth is that, for us, making love is something so intimate and pleasurable that we wouldn't change it for the ardor and passion of our younger days. It's difficult to explain but we just feel so very, very close to each other."

Life during these years presents extraordinary opportunities for a couple. They have more leisure time and they can start up new joint projects which are enjoyable and allow them to grow together. New family relationships arise: Sons and daughters-in-law, grandchildren ... and also relationships outside the family: Friends, companions and other couples who they did not have enough time to be with before, when their children were living at home.

Although there are some delicate points that we shall be explaining how to prevent or face in this chapter, this stage can become a source of great happiness and satisfaction.

How can we explain these findings? Most specialists coincide in their interpretations of the facts saying that the empty nest effect is two-sided, depending on the quality of a couple's relationship:

1. **The empty nest crisis: This affects certain marriages that were already suffering serious problems**. These couples choose to avoid getting divorced for their children's sakes. They live in an atmosphere of conflict for many years, trying to hide their problems from outsiders and from their children. Once the spouses find themselves alone, a break-up is inevitable.

2. **The relief of a roomy nest:** This happens in solid marriages which have enjoyed a healthy, balanced relationship over several decades. In these cases, their children's departure affords them an extraordinary opportunity to expand their relationship both in depth and breadth. Their children's self-sufficiency enables them to fully enjoy each other's company; something similar to a second honeymoon.

The term "empty nest syndrome" refers precisely to the stage we are concerned with. Once the children leave home to study, for professional reasons, to get married, or simply because of their desire for emancipation, certain symptoms may arise in one or both parents:

- Discomfort or tiredness for no apparent reason,
- A feeling of emptiness,
- Disorientation as regards family goals and objectives,
- Marital crisis,
- Signs of depression.

The fact of the matter is that the various studies carried out to confirm this belief have

been unable to demonstrate that the symptoms identified as pertaining to this so-called "syndrome" are true for a majority of cases. It is true, however, that a relatively high incidence of divorce exists during this stage. In fact, after the first 8 or 10 years of marriage, which shows the highest divorce rates, this stage attracts the next highest rates.

Therefore, attributing hidden, long-standing problems to their children's departure is a mistake which puts many couples unnecessarily on their guard. They may, under the misbelief that they are in imminent danger of breaking up, feel themselves pushed towards a crisis from the effect of this prejudice.

Positive Options in this stage

We propose looking to this stage confidently, assessing the variety of positive options that this new horizon opens up:

- An increase in free-time and the freedom to start up new activities separately or together.

- Mitigation from the work and worries associated with children living under their parents' roof.

- The opportunity to develop a wider social network.

- Greater economic means to carry out projects which were postponed, time and time again, due to lack of resources.

- Especially for the wife, freedom from the attitude of putting her children first all the time.

- For the wife who did not previously work outside the home, an opportunity to broaden her working horizons to do somehing which not only satisfies her, but also provides her with an income.

One of the new phenomena in industrialized countries is the boomerang effect. Strangely, after the supposed "trauma" of the children's departure, these often come back to live with their parents. The reason is eminently practical: once their studies or work contracts have ended, a son or a daughter will return home to live indefinitely until the next opportunity arises. The same applies to those children whose marriages fail; they return to their parents' home, sometimes with children of their own. Although parental love and commitment to their children extends to all inconveniences, such circumstances may obstruct a couple's personal development and place a moratorium on parents' plans.

On the other hand, being together for a long time and without children may highlight certain features of a partner's personality, which, in the past, had not posed a problem. This is the case of the talkative and silent spouses, as is demonstrated in the box "From the Psychologist's Desk" on page 65.

Better to prevent than to cure

There may be cases where even in a good marriage some empty nest crisis indicators are detected. This is common among parents given to overprotecting their children. Such parents employ a methodology whereby they occupy an over-caring and significant role in their children's lives, impeding them from making their own decisions.

To prevent problems in the face of our children's departure we have to accept that the parents' mission is to help their children mature and reach independence. This is a gradual but inevitable step in the human development process. We recommend two lines of action:

1. As children grow up in the heart of their family, allow them to make their own decisions (although still offering parental guidance) and to live with the consequences.

2. Once children live away from home, continue keeping up positive and friendly relations, but without trying to govern their lives and those of their new families.

This attitude will help parents to appreciate and accept the differences between their opinions, decisions, and behavior and those of their children.

The greatest number of marriage break-ups happen after 8 to 10 years of living together. The second danger period for the marriage is when the last child leaves the family home. Maggie Hayes studied this phenomenon to find out why people got divorced at this age and to thus discover ways of avoiding it (Hayes, M.P., 1979).

The predominant reasons are outlined below:

- Lack of contact, joint activities, dealings.
- Lack of communication and conversation at all levels.
- Imbalance of power, generally male domination.
- Absorption in work, especially on the part of the man.
- Unfaithfulness.
- Crises due to age (menopause, andropause).

Forestall the problems

To keep a marriage together and satisfied, we advise the following:

- **Set priorities for the couple**. While giving the family, work, etc. the time that corresponds to them, spouses should have special, fixed occasions for being together and carrying out joint activities. This should be on their list of priorities.

- **Consider the principle of equality as a goal**. Both spouses should consider themselves important in the relationship; both should feel they possess sufficient authority.

- **Keep a balance between personal growth and that of the couple**. Individualism should not be allowed to overcome a married couple's unity. However, it is also dangerous to melt personalities to such an extent that no individual identity remains.

- **Maintain a sex life based on quality**. Sex for a middle-aged couple is positive but requires a certain measure of effort and planning.

- **Meet up with other couples**. Now with more time and freedom, deeper friendships can be forged with couples who, like yourselves, are working to make a success of their marriage.

- **Add some "spark" to your marriage**. Some people consider a change of partner a good way of adding spark to their lives. It is much better to liven up a relationship through a change in one's lifestyle, or by doing something new with one's companion.

- **Prevent unfaithfulness**. The key to a happy marriage is that both partners find satisfaction within their relationship. The next chapter offers some advice for achieving this, in the box entitled "How to stay faithful" on page 82.

"My husband hardly speaks to me"

I am very talkative and, as is natural, I like to chat with my husband. Now our children no longer live with us, he and I should talk much more to each other ... However, when he comes home from work, he talks for a while and then he goes and reads or does some paperwork. And sometimes two or three days will go by without us talking together. Then we go back to normal, that is, some talking, but only a little. What can I do to make him talk more?

It is very possible that your husband is not very talkative by nature and it requires a greater effort for him to hold a conversation than it does for you. On the other hand, men tend to use fewer words than women. Some studies have shown that the mean number of words a woman uses daily is 25,000, while a man uses some 12,500.

Furthermore, tastes in conversation vary considerably between men and women. Women prefer to speak about subjective, personal matters: their perception of things, their opinion on what their friends, family, neighbors, celebrities etc. do. However, men prefer to chat about objective, impersonal topics: Politics, sports, social problems and so on.

You should therefore moderate your expectations. Nevertheless, here is some advice:

- **Do not harass him, asking or begging him to talk more**. Sometimes people, and especially men, try to resolve something which is troubling them psychologically by keeping quiet. This may be your husband's case during those two or three days he goes without speaking, before returning to normality. Do not force the situation during those moments.

- **Get him out of the house to foster conversation**. Suggest going for a walk, wherever he likes most, so that he feels relaxed and he will take part in the conversation.

- **Find out which topics please him most**. Bring up his preferred topics. It is difficult for a person who is sparing with words to participate in conversations which he finds tedious.

- **Take advantage of an appropriate moment to talk about the problem**. Ask him why he some-times stays silent. Suggest his silence may be due to a problem or annoyance. Assure him you are willing to help. If you manage to find out his reasons it will be much easier for you to live with him.

- **And when you do finally manage to get him to speak a little more**, feel happy and show your satisfaction so that he will continue to progress.

Middle age (40 – 65 year-old age group) has been compared with adolescence (12 – 18 year-old age group). Both have to face pressure, changes and alternatives but they also have multiple opportunities and a wide range of options with interesting outlets.

A crisis may be unleashed by ...

Indeed, couples at this vital stage have to face a number of challenges which may unleash a crisis:

1. **Their children leaving home**. For two decades or more, the couple have devoted the greater part of their endeavors and resources to their children. From their earliest childhood when they required constant physical care up to when they study, go to work or choose a spouse, the parents have participated fully, until their children have gone away to live by themselves. Once this effort comes to an end, mothers and fathers ask themselves what their new aim in life is.

2. **Menopause and andropause**. Hormonal changes in men and women result in changes in their sexuality, in their emotional lives and in their physique ... This reminds the couple of their age and the fact that they have passed the midpoint in their lives.

3. **The risk of marital instability**. For many couples, and especially those whose past relationship has been troubled, this stage may set off a marriage crisis. When they are left alone, their differences, abruptness and frustrations are all uncovered and the couple will pass through difficult times.

4. **The loss of parents**. Many couples of this age have to live through the previous generation's concluding years. The passing away of parents and parents-in-law is a stressful experience in itself. And if it comes as the result of a long illness which has required great physical and psychological effort, grief joins hands with the accumulated strain and is even more difficult to accept.

A stage full of new opportunities

Luckily these aspects may be prepared for, confronted and resolved. Roger Gould is one of the pioneers in research into the middle age stage of human development, and he concludes that it is a time of satisfaction and acceptance of personal achievements (Gould, R.L., 1975, 1979, and 1993). This stage offers many attractive opportunities for a couple:

1. **A liberating situation**. The departure of their children need not provoke a crisis. Rather it should engender a feeling of liberation and of a phase now concluded. Sending their children off to live

their own lives is the culmination of years of effort and dedication; clearly an achievement. Now the couple are more mobile, and have more time, money and stability in their home. It is the moment for carrying out those projects together, trips, dreams … which were impossible to do in the past.

2. **A stage filled with pleasure and intimacy**. Menopause and andropause should not be a barrier within the marital relationship. Completely the opposite; husband and wife need to feel they are lovers as they did when they were newly wed. Family planning, menstruation, the busy and worrying times the children brought, have all been left behind … With our life expectancy today, a fifty-year-old can well hope for a further thirty years of happy marriage. It is therefore the moment to bring hopes and plans back into the marriage.

3. **A stage of stability**. Although for those in problematic relationships, their marriage will be put under a severe test, couples whose relationships are built on solid foundations not only stay together after their children leave home, but gain in stability and personal satisfaction.

4. **A family rejuvenation**. Although the loss of parents and parents-in-law implies a painful experience, the arrival of grandchildren is a source of immense satisfaction. This stage also opens new horizons in family relationships. It is the time to broaden and deepen relations with one's children and their spouses; to help and guide them in solving their problems and in sketching out plans for their own and their children's futures. They also have more time to explore other family relationships. And regarding other social ties, middle-aged

couples are presented with the opportunity of making new friends, especially with people of similar age, who are also in the throes of the emotional task of building up their marriages.

In summary, we should acknowledge that we can consider this time in a couple's life from two different angles. Middle age can be a troubled and perplexing time … but it may also turn into an enjoyable experience, full of opportunities for the couple. It depends on the choices we make.

In preparation for this marvelous stage, we invite the reader to discover the reasons why marriages fail after the children leave home and also to follow the advice offered which will help strengthen their marriage during these years.

An important aspect to bear in mind is communication between the couple. We saw previously in chapter 3, the guidelines for fostering good communication in general. Now, at this advanced stage in the relationship, the most intricate details of the husband-wife dialog should be examined. The box "What do you think about when people are talking to you", shows how a listener's attitude can significantly affect the dialog.

Children leave home at various ages depending on individual circumstances or on cultural traditions. Nevertheless, most couples find their children leave home when parents are between 45 and 55 years old.

This age is marked by the onset of important physical changes. These alterations usually begin gradually. Therefore, one is not aware of any significant loss.

Keenness of sight and hearing

There is a loss of visual keenness in the following areas:

- Near sight,
- Viewing moving objects or messages,
- Night vision,
- Visual search amid other stimuli,
- The speed of processing visual information.

Although there is great variation between one person and another, these changes begin between the ages of 40 and 50, reaching a loss of some importance (requiring some sort of corrective measure) at the age of 60. The use of progressive lenses is more comfortable, as one does not need to be constantly changing glasses for different functions.

The aural capacity

There is also a gradual loss of hearing, which accelerates between the ages of 50 and 60. it is estimated that by retirement age, 25% of the population has suffered a significant loss of hearing (Merrill, S.S. and Verbrugge, L.M., 1999). The incidence is twice as high among men as it is in women. This problem can be partly prevented by avoiding exposing oneself to very loud sounds, or by using protective ear-plugs or ear-phones when noise is unavoidable. The aural health of young people today is at greater risk than in previous generations, because they often listen to music at full volume and attend live performances of musical groups (Wallhagen, M.I. et al, 1997).

Smell and taste

Our senses of smell and taste lose their accuracy little by little. This implies that as people approach retirement age they find food less tasty. The capacity

The characteristics and symptoms listed in this box are not experienced by all middle-aged men and women. In fact, most only experience these hormone changes to a lesser degree. Menopause and andropause signal the beginning for the couple of a greater freedom in their sexual relations, without running the risk of pregnancy. At the same time, these developments coincide with the departure of their children and spouses feel a greater sense of freedom overall.

Menopause (Female)

The organism reduces secretions of estrogen and progesterone which sometimes leads to the following symptoms:

- Hot flashes
- Urinary difficulties
- Irritability
- Headaches
- Symptoms of depression
- Vaginal dryness
- A loss of fertility
- An increase in body weight
- The risk of osteoporosis

Andropause (Male)

The organism reduces secretions of androgen and testosterone, which sometimes leads to the following symptoms:

- Anxiety
- Irritability
- Sleeplessness
- Fatigue
- Loss of memory
- Symptoms of depression
- A drop in fertility
- A reduction in muscle and bone mass
- Balding

to distinguish bitter, salty, spicy and acid flavors begins to weaken, however we continue to be able to savor sweet tasting foods. People should be warned not to fall into undesirable nutritional habits, such as seasoning food with too much salt or spice to bring out more flavor. Our sense of taste can be educated by exposing it to simple flavors for a prolonged time period, until the nerve endings transmit the precise message to the taste center in our brain.

Our various psychomotor functions start to become affected at this age. Our co-ordination and muscular strength begin to decline after the age of 30, but the decrease is unperceivable. However, between 45 and 60, ten percent of these faculties are lost. (Merrill, S.S. and Verbrugge, L.M., 1999). As our body is now composed of 20% or more of fat (as opposed to 10% in adolescence), a low-fat diet accompanied by physical exercise may slow this loss down for many years.

Physical endurance

Physical endurance also decreases, but in line with our strength at the same age. For example, an athlete who has done a ten-kilometer run every day for many years, need not feel more tired at the age of 60. The secret lies in not letting these habits drop.

Reflexes

Our reflexes fall quite considerably (around 20% by the time we reach 60). However, our general ability to carry out duties requiring the use of our reflexes does not decline, especially if we have been practicing these regularly. For example a good 20-year-old typist is no better than one aged 60. The same happens when it comes to driving a motor vehicle or operating machinery. This loss of reflexes is understood to be compensated by long experience which equips the person to accurately predict movements.

Menopause and andropause

Menopause is a compulsory step for all women reaching middle age, and is termed andropause when describing the equivalent process in a man. It is marked by **hormonal changes** (see the box on the previous page). These result in **physical and psychological changes** in most people, and produce significant effects in a minority (approximately 10% of the population).

For women it is considered to be a precise point in time, one year after their last menstruation, normally between the ages of 45 and 55, the average being 51. These changes are much less exact and present greater variation in men.

Tradition and publicity have overemphasized the negative aspects of menopause. According to this disparaging view, every woman could expect to be shaken by severe changes in her physiology and be subjected to constant psychological strain.

Actually, most women contemplate menopause as a transition and not a crisis or illness. Despite many experiencing the symptoms listed in the box on the previous page, this does not upset their marital, social or professional relations. What is more, many women consider this step as a relief from menstruation and fertility, while not having to renounce their sex lives.

A normal process

How does the data offered so far affect our health overall? The reply is encouraging. The variations we have described are part of a normal developmental process, and except in certain cases, should not affect our normal lives as far as work, social lives, and relationship with a partner go.

Nevertheless, there are health risks in middle age. We are referring to heart disease, stroke, and cancer. These often fatal diseases have much to do with **lifestyle**.

It is therefore extremely important to take the basic health principles seriously: A simple, balanced, healthy diet, regular physical exercise, water and fresh air, abstention from tobacco, alcohol and other drugs, sufficient rest and peace of mind.

- Changes experienced by men
- The quantity of semen decreases.
- The force of ejaculation declines.
- The testicles become smaller and less firm.
- Erections are less frequent and not so hard.
- Orgasms take longer to arrive.

Many surveys have shown that sexual encounters in middle-aged couples improve in comparison with those of previous stages. Indeed, the worries of an unwanted pregnancy, interruptions caused by children living at home, and lack of time suppose important barriers to a full and complete sex life. Now, without such obstacles, sexuality takes on a more prominent and satisfactory role.

However, we should remember that, in middle age, there are certain physiological changes in the structure and function of the sex organs.

Changes experienced by women

- Sexual excitement is not so intense.
- An orgasm is less frequent and less prolonged.
- The vulva loses consistency.
- The vagina contracts and its elasticity diminishes.
- Vaginal lubrication declines during intercourse.

These changes appear gradually over several years which facilitates their assimilation. As a result of these changes, the number of sexual encounters may decrease slightly. However, as far as quality is concerned, this need not decrease at all.

For couples who have been sexually active for **20 or 30 years**, this stage can be satisfactory. It is women who notice the **greatest improvement** in their sex lives, (as long as there is a good marital relationship). At this age women are fully aware of their own sexual needs and because of their maturity they are able to express them more openly to their partner.

They feel better able to initiate sexual play, and given that their partners are less rushed or impatient, their sexual encounters can be extended.

Furthermore, as men at this age take longer to reach their orgasm, women find it easier to reach their own orgasm, which always requires a longer build-up.

In conclusion, if we understand sex as not merely a means of procreation, but also a means of expressing and enjoying ourselves, we can find that sexuality at this stage fulfills the one role of bringing couples closer in pleasure and mutual enjoyment. This situation opens up new opportunities and horizons to be explored in the sex lives of couples whose children have left home.

Charles and Patty have been married for 25 years and have older children living away from home. Their relationship has always been healthy. Patty is a very capable woman but she tends **to feel insecure**, due precisely to her low level of self-esteem, which has worsened since her children left; she no longer feels so useful and essential as she did when her children lived at home.

When she is in a group situation, even if she knows the other people, she finds it very difficult to speak. If she is asked a question she gets nervous and sometimes blushes. Her husband sometimes silently wonders: "Why does she go to pieces, stammering when she speaks to people, if she never does that with me or in a smaller group?"

One night they stayed up late talking. Patty brought up the topic of her insecurity, but she could not pinpoint the reason for her problem. She did say that she was afraid of showing her ignorance, and she mentioned that she **feared** being in the limelight, because people would realize how rounded her hips were.

Charles, amazed by her reasoning, sincerely assured her that he held her as an intelligent woman who he always trusted when it came to making important decisions; that things had always gone well in the family thanks to her initiative and clarity of mind. As far as her hips were concerned, Charles stated that these were just figments of her imagination. They spoke about these matters on other occasions and Patty began to feel better.

The effect of these "therapeutic sessions" was not long in coming. The next time they met up with their friends Patty began talking in a balanced and untroubled way.

Through this experience Charles discovered that *the concept one has of oneself is influenced by others*. With great care, he undertook to make **positive comments** here and there and he observed how Patty quickly shook off her insecurities astonishingly quickly.

Possessing an adequate level of self-esteem, or, on the contrary, living under the belief that one is inferior, **can have a decisive effect on a marriage. People with adequate self-esteem**:

- Possess a greater facility for interpersonal relations,
- Possess a greater capacity for communication,
- Are less susceptible to being hurt by outside criticism and
- Are less preoccupied that people hold them in poor esteem.

For their part, **the partner with a poor concept of him or herself,**

The building of self-esteem differs considerably for men and women. This is due fundamentally to social pressures. Although equality between men and women is being achieved in some twenty countries, over 90% of the world population lives in circumstances which do not allow women to occupy a relevant role in their communities. It is here that the husband's role in building his wife's self-esteem takes on special significance.

In women

- Through professional activities, although in many societies the opportunities to do so are limited.
- Through bringing up children and household duties.
- By means of their close friends and family and also their work colleagues.
- Through their beauty (versus their intelligence).
- Through their husbands' influence as they take on an outstanding role in the development of their wives' self-esteem.

In men

- Through the exercise of their trade or profession.
- A successful professional tends to feel good about himself.
- Through the influence of colleagues, clients, superiors, and subordinates.
- Through their intelligence (versus their physical attractiveness).
- Through their wives' actions, although this usually takes a secondary position compared with professional aspects..

has **an insatiable need for affection** and doubts that his or her companion's love is real.

The type of relationship a couple has is directly linked to their quality of self-esteem. The box on page 43 describes the typology proposed by Crosby. Here it is seen that the most desirable marital relationship is that of interdependence, based on mutual support and both partners having a healthy self-esteem.

Many areas of a couple's lives are affected by appropriate levels of self esteem. Below we have outlined the most outstanding:

1. **Everyday duties**. A wife, who is sincerely praised by her husband will feel encouraged and strong enough to carry out all her duties properly. In the same way, a husband who is admired by his wife is most likely to succeed in his obligations.

2. **Care in attentions toward each other**. The small touches of affection and attention between partners are decisive elements for making a success of living together. But these simple actions are made more difficult when there are feelings of inferiority. Thus a vicious circle begins whereby little love for oneself impedes demonstrations of love to one's partner.

3. **Sexuality**. A woman with low self-esteem feels she is being exploited and believes that the sole aim of their sexual relations is to satisfy her partner's desires. She also tends to feel guilty and unworthy when she receives sexual satisfaction. For his part, a man with a poor self-concept wishes to compensate his inferiority by proving how virile he is.

4. **Marital abuse or mistreatment**. Often, when a man feels inferior he acts violently toward his wife to obtain greater control and to achieve a feeling of power and domination over her. For her part, the wife/victim, if she possesses low self-esteem, will acquiesce to such treatment because she believes, in her heart of hearts, that she deserves nothing better.

5. **Jealousy**. Poor self-esteem and personal insecurity in many cases give rise to unfounded jealousy. Only those who feel inferior end up being obsessed with their partners being unfaithful to them.

6. **The perception of oneself**. A partner who feels ugly and clumsy, may not actually be so, but his or her belief leads to behavior which may complicate a relationship.

Circle the number which best fits your experience, following the key below

N – Never   AN – Almost Never   F – Frequently   AA – Almost Always   A – Always

	Never			Always	
	N	AN	F	AA	A
1. Although I do not consider myself to be physically perfect, I feel satisfied with my appearance.	0	1	2	3	4
2. When I contemplate a physically attractive model, actor, actress and so on, I feel inferior.	4	3	2	1	0
3. Although susceptible to improvement, I am happy with my problem-solving capacity.	0	1	2	3	4
4. I think that I am slow and clumsy when it comes to providing solutions to difficulties.	4	3	2	1	0
5. When a job I do is well done, I am able to recognize my personal effort and value.	0	1	2	3	4
6. If something I do turns out well, I think it is due to help received from others or simply a stroke of luck.	4	3	2	1	0
7. When my plans fail, I avoid blaming myself but rather look for explanations to the cause and incidents outside of my control.	0	1	2	3	4
8. When my plans fail, I consider myself solely responsible for their failure.	4	3	2	1	0
9. When I deal with my companions/colleagues I feel equal to them.	0	1	2	3	4
10. I tend to feel inferior to my companions and friends.	4	3	2	1	0
11. I understand there are people who enjoy my company and value my qualities.	0	1	2	3	4
12. I get the feeling that when people visit me they do so out of politeness and not because they really enjoy my company.	4	3	2	1	0
13. It pleases me to receive sincere praise from others.	0	1	2	3	4
14. When others praise me for a job well done, I hurry to contradict them and their praises make me feel guilty.	4	3	2	1	0
15. I try to keep good memories of the past and avoid worrying about the future.	0	1	2	3	4
16. Adverse situations from the past bother me, and I look to the future with uncertainty.	4	3	2	1	0
17. If I express my personal values and principles to others, I do so easily and without embarrassment.	0	1	2	3	4
18. When I speak to others about my ideas and opinions, I am afraid they will reject me if they do not think as I do.	4	3	2	1	0

INTERPRETATION

To find out your level of self-esteem, add up your total number of points scored. Below is the interpretation corresponding to the different score ranges:

If you scored UNDER 32 ... your level of self-esteem is very low.. You really need to revise your capabilities and your achievements and recognize your personal values. Leaving things as they are will result in suffering in the areas of your personal satisfaction, your work and your relationships. Seek help, and trust in a friend or a mental health professional to get out of this situation.

If you scored BETWEEN 32 AND 41 ... your level of self-esteem is poor and it is necessary to try to enrich it by distancing yourself from those who criticize and scorn you, seeking instead the company of those who appreciate you. Perhaps your spouse is partly contributing to this situation. Speak to him or her at the right moment and lay out your worries; encourage him or her to make more constructive comments.

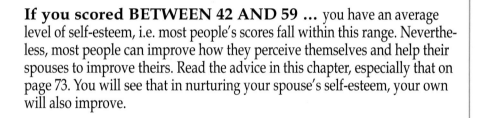

If you scored BETWEEN 42 AND 59 ... you have an average level of self-esteem, i.e. most people's scores fall within this range. Nevertheless, most people can improve how they perceive themselves and help their spouses to improve theirs. Read the advice in this chapter, especially that on page 73. You will see that in nurturing your spouse's self-esteem, your own will also improve.

If you scored BETWEEN 60 AND 68 ... you can consider you possess a healthy self-esteem, without complexes and without doubts about yourself. Be careful, however, in not stepping over the line into arrogance or self-sufficiency.

If you scored OVER 68 ... perhaps you are in a delicate situation due the extreme nature of your score. It is desirable to have a good self-concept , but when it is touching perfection it is advisable to take a dose of humility because, when all is said and done, nobody is perfect.

Crisis within the couple

Chapter Summary

Charles and Patricia have been married for five years. Each has their own job and their own professional aims, and in this respect everything seems to be going well. But when they are at home, they have big fights.

Charles complains that his wife is too sensitive and emotional; she places great importance on trivial things and small details … He would like her to be open and direct in saying what she wants, instead of expecting him to read her mind. Moreover, Patricia's relationship with her mother puts him at his wits' end.

She, on the other hand, sees her husband as a fundamentally dominant man. He tries to control her in everything she does. He criticizes her because she has friends; he scolds her for talking on the telephone. And furthermore, he becomes obsessed every time it comes to spending money: "Why do we want another lamp? What's wrong with the one we've got at home?"

During their lives together, many couples go through problems; some simple, others serious. This chapter examines some of these marriage problems. We explain the nature of these conflicts, their possible causes, and solutions which may be of interest.

Life as a couple **today** involves a series of **specific problems** which may partly explain the reason for marital unfaithfulness:

- A lifestyle lacking serenity has become increasingly common where high levels of **generalized stress** are registered. Competitive posts with strong demands on production, high economic requirements, the urgency inherent in the tasks, etc., put people under strain which is then transferred into their family lives. Thus, certain adverse attitudes, such as propensity to anger, may disrupt a couple's stability.

- **Lack of time** is one of the main causes of marital imbalance and break-ups. The marriage commitment requires an investment in terms of time. Couples devote many hours to their jobs throughout the week, leaving duties unfinished. All of this forms an important barrier when it comes to nourishing a relationship.

- Where there are **children**, they require special attention as seen in chapter 4. Today many options are available ranging from nurseries to university courses. And apart from their studies, we must not forget free-time activities and the development of values. Attending to these demands is expensive, not only in financial terms, but also as regards the time and effort involved.

- The **expectations that partners** have of marriage are much higher and demanding than ever before. Their roles are no longer fixed and it is not enough for the husband to be the breadwinner and the wife to take care of the home and children. Nowadays, many people demand multiple satisfactions from marriage. When these expectations are not fulfilled, partners begin to consider the breakup option.

- **Decision-making** is no longer a male prerogative. Many couples share authority. This is liberating for the oppressed party (usually, the wife), but it can also be a source of conflict, especially when one of the parties is not satisfied.

- The **media**, including Internet, are opening up enormous opportunities which carry advantages but also the risk of limiting interpersonal communication and complicating life in a relationship.

- If we add to these factors such issues as **violence, drugs, alcohol and the absence of ethical and spiritual values**, we find our-

  - selves with a growing number of couples who come to the conclusion that their marriage is not worthwhile. As a consequence they seek happiness outside their relationship and usually do not find it.

77

On other occasions, however, a couple who wishes to find a solution is more than capable of finding it for themselves.

Given that it is practically impossible to find a conflict-free couple, we should ask ourselves the question: How can we resolve conflicts in a civilized manner? Many husbands will agree that it is harder to negotiate with their wives over some household issue than to carry out negotiations for an important commercial contract. The fundamental reason is that when there is intimacy in the negotiation it becomes charged with sentiment and emotion. This may be beneficial when there is no conflict. But in order to resolve problems and troubles, a dose of logic is required, which is incompatible with feelings.

- Despite all we have said so far, we should underline **that crises can play a unifying and strengthening role**. When a marriage has faced sizeable difficulties over several decades, the couple is much stronger and more united. Serious incidents such as the death of a child, loss of employment, illness, bankruptcy … have converted many marriages into unmovable anchors where loyalty and unity prevail.

Is it possible to find a couple who do not argue?

It is unlikely. In fact, the happiest couples are precisely those who know how to argue without psychologically ripping their spouses apart.

The couples who split up for extreme reasons such as violence, unfaithfulness, the use of alcohol and drugs and so on, are in fact, a minority. Many separations and divorces are due to the onset of conflicts and the couples' inability to find a solution.

Sometimes, even though the problems encountered have a clear and reasonable solution, the couple is without sufficient emotional reserves to resolve the conflict. In such cases they need a neutral outsider (a marriage counselor, for example) who can lead them, step by step, towards a solution to their problem.

Many specialists in marriage therapy employ the following steps to resolve conflicts between a couple. By means of negotiation, in which neither spouse attains a hundred per cent of what he or she wants, it is possible that both reach a reasonable level of satisfaction.

1. **Understanding the problem well**. Many couples become engaged in serious fights without really knowing what they want or appreciating their spouses' perspective. The primordial task is to learn from one's partner by actively listening. To confirm that they have understood each other, both partners need to repeat the problem as seen through the eyes of their spouse. For fur-ther detail, see the box "To become a better listener" in chapter three, page 40.

2. **Specify each partner's wishes**. This is a step of utmost importance because it helps couples to concentrate on their aims instead of on their complaints. Both partners there-fore need to express what it is they want as far as the problem is concerned. The more concrete the wishes are, the easier it is to negotiate them. For instance, it is better to say: "When we're with friends I'd like you not to joke about me being a manic cleaner and changing the sheets twice a week," than saying: I'd like you to be more respectful towards me when we're in the company of others."

3. **Explore various options**. It is the moment to propose solutions. This is not the time to opt for one definitive route, but rather one for laying out possibilities or multiple options from which a best alternative may be drawn. For example, solutions to a complaint about excessive or un-equal relations with respective parents-in-law would be:

   a. For each visit we make to your parents, we will make one to mine.

   b. Limit family visits of every kind to two per year.

   c. When one spouse speaks to his/her mo-ther or father on the telephone, the other spouse should not be forced to get on and hold a long conversation.

   d. Speak to both families and describe frankly and respectfully the manner in which we would like to develop our relations with them.

4. **Negotiate**. The moment has come to reach a sufficiently balanced solution that will satisfy both spouses. It is fitting to find some middle point in the negotiation, either by sharing the load which will be incumbent in the solution, or by trading off wishes ("I won't protest when you spend small amounts, but you mustn't nag when I go fishing with my friends"). These types of agreements leave both parties with the feeling that they have obtained some satisfaction, be it only partial. In the worse cases, if no agreement is reached, the spouses at least agree to disagree: Mandy and Richard are in dissent as to what to do with their savings. Mandy wants to go on a cruise and Richard to pay the deposit on a condominium. As they could not agree, it was decided that the money should stay in the bank until negotiations resumed. And in the meantime, they agree not to quarrel any more.

5. **Reassert agreements**. It is very important to work hard in the negotiation, because once a pact is made, the agreement and mutual responsibilities must be kept. When one partner breaches the agreement, this will generate a spirit of deception and lack of confidence making the next negotiation more difficult. Writing agreements in contract form, making a serious verbal declaration to each other or using an arbitrator-witness are successfully employed in marriage therapy.

6. **Make periodic reviews**. An agreement made in theory is not always viable when put into practice. Therefore, most pacts made by a couple need to be reviewed periodically. In this way adjustments may be achieved, enabling the agreement to continue. At the end of the day, the objective is to completely do without agreements and to live a reasonably happy relationship.

Personal style in conflictresolution

Besides following a method as described above, in order to buffer the emotional aspects involved in negotiation, one's personal style of conflict resolution has to be taken into account. Kilmann and Thomas identified the following styles (Kilmann, R. and Thomas, K., 1975):

- **The competitive style** consists of taking control in applying a solution to the conflict. It may be efficient as it is strongly solution-oriented, but is poor in recognizing outside needs. It is especially dangerous when both partners in a couple are competitive.

- **The collaborative style**, probably the most recommended, is that belonging to an active person who seeks to find a mutually valid solution. In the choice of solutions, the person bears in mind his or her partner's needs, and thus is more likely to find a satisfactory outcome. Although this style requires effort due to its strong negotiation component, it is attainable.

- **The compromise style**, includes both parties and its application is simple. In this instance, the person has sufficient assertiveness and a good level of sensitivity towards his or her partner's needs. The aim in the conflict solution is for both parties to make equal concessions so there is neither a winner nor a loser. It is a fair system, but may prove unsatisfactory for resolving complex problems where it is impossible to find the exact midway point.

- **The avoidance style** is an attitude characterized by little thrust in a solution and little sensitivity towards others' needs. It involves forgetting the problem, not thinking about the conflict, putting the matter aside and waiting for things to improve. The main disadvantage with this method is that most conflicts do not easily disappear and often reappear later with more intensity.

- **The accommodating style** is dominated by adaptation to the other partner's needs, but with little initiative to face the conflict. The accommodating person sacrifices his or her desires to avoid colliding with a partner's. In practice, a spouse who concedes time and time again eventually tires and demands his or her spouse to correspond in kind. A further inconvenience is the absence of dialog and negotiation, depriving the couple of this necessary practice in order to reach new agreements and pacts.

Infidelity is the breach of one's marriage vows, which commit a man and a woman to live together renouncing all others. In North America it is estimated that 21% of men and 11% of women are unfaithful at some time in their lives (National Opinion Research Center, 1994). It is possible that the level is, in fact, much higher. After all, those who are capable of deceiving their spouses are also capable of lying in a survey.

It is strange that in countries which enjoy the freedom of whether or not to get married, or of divorce, infidelity is frequent. This may be explained by the extra satisfaction obtained through maintaining a secret love affair, with its touch of danger.

The history of most infidelities follows the following **pattern**:

1. The marriage enters a *state of monotony* or lacks some ingredient which is considered essential.

2. *Someone crosses one of the spouses' paths* and shows interest and pays compliments.

3. The third person's presence begins to feel pleasant and *takes the spouse back to the times when he or she first felt in love*: "So-and-so understands me, he/she takes me as I am, with affection and unconditionally …"

4. The first *signs of sincere love* appear on both sides ending up with mutual promises: "I'll get divorced as soon as I can and we'll get married."

5. A *parallel life* sets in with an exchange of emotional, sexual and practical favors.

6. After a variable length of time the novelty wears off; the early passion dries up and is overcome by the *arguments and routines* of every relationship. It is here that the question arises of whether or not it is worthwhile continuing.

7. If the love affair has not been discovered by the spouse, the unfaithful party discretely "*returns*" to the official marital relationship. If he or she has been discovered, they ask for forgiveness and promise to be faithful in the future. In time there may or may not be further episodes of unfaithfulness.

Apart from the most visible aspects of an extramarital affair (sex, mutual companionship, enjoyable conversation) there is an underpinning root to the whole process: the need for both men and women to *satisfy their ego and to nourish their self-esteem*. When such positive messages as: "How beautiful you look!" "You really are a strong and self-controlled man." "Your cleverness surprises me," are no longer used in a marriage but are heard from outside, they seem to act like a magnet to the human being. King Solomon, in the Book of Proverbs, devoted chapter seven to the description of a seduction. It is precisely the woman's words of praise which finally bring the man down: *"With much seductive speech she persuades him; with her smooth talk she compels him."* (Proverbs 7: 21).

HOW TO KEEP UP A FAITHFUL RELATIONSHIP

In a society which tolerates (or even to a certain extent promotes) unfaithfulness, its incidence will tend to rise. However, the real root of unfaithfulness goes beyond the license awarded by society. A relationship in which both spouses obtain emotional, intellectual, social and physical satisfaction is the best way to assure faithfulness. If, on the other hand, a relationship lacks the minimum resources, one (or both) of the spouses may opt for other alternatives. Benjamin Franklin's phrase, "Where there is a marriage without love, there will be love without marriage", is sufficient to understand the principle.

We have listed below some effective advice to maintain a faithful marriage:

- **Be honest in all areas of one's marriage**. An open, honest relationship is one in which there is no room for lies, even over the smallest details. This constitutes a serious impediment to extra-marital affairs behind a spouse's back.

- **Keep the couple's circle closed**. The problems and conflicts which arise within a couple are exclusive to the couple. With the exception of pathological aspects (violence, illness) requiring the help of a third person, these problems should be discussed behind closed doors. Infidelity sometimes makes its way in when someone hears one partner complaining about the other.

- **Fan the flames of romance.** Making an effort to keep a relationship meaningful and lively is basic and crucial. One should not be ashamed of going back to the habits of one's youth: going out together, sending love-letters, giving presents, giving an unexpected kiss and above all, devoting time to talking and doing things together.

- **Keeping up a good sex life**. Although this is not the only reason for unfaithfulness, it is often the case for men who are dissatisfied with their marital sex lives. Time should be put aside to explore new ways of satisfying each other sexually, and keeping up a vibrant and exciting sex life. Make every effort to keep a partner sexually satisfied.

- **Attend to nourishing self-esteem**. The messages of approval that were sent during courtship and the first stage of marriage do not last forever. A human being needs to periodically feed his/her ego. This requires sincere and suitable praise. Most men enjoy receiving compliments about their physical strength, their hard work and their intelligence. Women are nurtured by sensitive words and gestures of praise about their physical attractiveness, their problem-solving capacity and their sweet, affectionate nature. When these areas are undernourished, a man or a woman ends up falling into a lover's arms.

Unfounded jealousy is an emotion which arises out of a disproportionate attempt to possess a spouse or loved one in an exclusive, all-absorbing way. It can also be understood as an ingrained fear of losing a loved one through his/her love of another person. In a married couple, jealousy centers on a possible sexual infidelity, but it is not always constrained to this. For example, a wife may feel jealous of her husband's work, because his job is absorbing and takes time away from their relationship. Or a husband may feel jealous of his children due to his wife's devotion and dedication towards them.

Jealousy is justified, when, in a situation of a promised faithfulness, one of the spouses decides to leave the relationship to be with ano-ther person. The abandoned spouse may feel jealous of the person who has robbed them of their loved one. But this usually ends either in reconciliation or break-up. However, when we speak of jealousy in a couple we are generally referring to unfounded jealousy, accompanied by distrust, harassment and suspicion, all of which represent a risk to a couple's happiness.

Where jealousy leads

In practice, jealousy always implies adverse processes and outcomes. Here are some of these:

- Jealousy may be accompanied by feelings which contribute to a lack of emotional stability in the jealous party: Anger, fear, insecurity, distrust, psychological pain. It may thus be the cause (or outcome) of emotional imbalance.

- Jealousy is a risk factor in a relationship. A couple, in which one of the members is jealous, is in a constant state of alarm and may fall out of love and break up.

- Jealousy is a significant emotional load for the jealous partner. A wife, for example, whose husband suffers unfounded jealousy, is deprived of her freedom and initiative, and feels constantly pressured by threats and "evidence" which indicate her infidelity.

- Jealousy is no guarantee of faithfulness nor of love on the part of the jealous spouse, but rather the opposite, as jealous partners show a greater tendency towards being unfaithful, than those who are not. This is perhaps due to the jealous partner's reasoning of: "If he/she is unfaithful, then I will do the same."

The reasons for jealousy

The origin of jealousy is unclear. Some evidence points to environmental or **social origins**. Anthropological research shows cultures which rank highly on a jealousy scale, such as the North American Apaches, and low jealousy ranking cultures such as those in the South of the Indian Subcontinent. The former show high levels of jealousy because their society places the utmost value on fidelity and considers any breach of this rule as a blight on their honor. This atmosphere seems to push both men and women into a state of constant alert to guard their respective spouses. In low jealousy-ranking cultures, how-ever, feelings of jealousy are rare because these societies are more tolerant of changes in partnerships.

Other studies associate jealousy to **features inherent in certain people**. There is a correlation between jealous behavior and certain personality features such as insecurity, self-criticism or paranoia. These findings have led many people to think that jealousy is rooted more in the person than in society, and thus they conclude that those who are naturally fearful, insecure with poor self-esteem and feelings of distrust are more likely to show jealous behavior.

The fact of the matter is, that while its origin is far from clear, it would seem obvious that both factors, personal and social, will contribute to this tendency to a greater or lesser degree.

How to control jealousy

From the psychotherapeutic viewpoint, helping a jealous spouse proves very difficult if he or she is really convinced of a partner's unfaithfulness, up to the point of harboring real delusions based on unfounded evidence. In the case of those who are aware of their suspicious nature and want to receive support, there are techniques which can provide definitive help, such as:

- **Thought control**. Jealous partners attend individual counseling sessions in which their jealous thoughts and the way in which their mind reaches and anchors such thoughts are examined. They are taught how to stop or divert those undesirable thoughts in order to systematically avoid them.

- **Behavioral plans**. Jealousy tends to sustain itself very effectively. The aim is therefore to identify habits, stimuli and reinforcing elements which perpetuate this behavior in order to eliminate them. There is reading material, certain company, places etc. which may induce jealous thoughts and these have to be avoided. A submissive attitude on the part of the accused spouse, may also fan the flames of jealousy.

- **Enhancing one's self-concept**. It is often one's poor self-concept that provokes jealousy; the person who feels inferior believes that anyone can enrapture his/her spouse. Therefore, patients receive training in how to improve their self-concept. This will provide them with the necessary self-confidence to stop suspecting their spouses of unfaithfulness.

- **Therapy for the couple**. Both partners in the couple receive the corresponding psychotherapy in which they speak openly and follow guidelines to foster greater confidence in one another. They also agree on prevention phases (advice for avoiding the problem) and they set consequences when jealous behavior reappears.

Over the last few years public opinion has become aware of a common yet hidden problem: Violence within the couple and the family. It has always existed, but before it was excused whereas today it is rejected in many societies.

What constitutes violence behind closed doors? It can be seen in the two ways outlined below:

- **Physical aggression**, which consists of pushing, slapping, scratching, punching or hitting with an object, causing burns or raping the victim (even a wife). It is generally the man who commits violent acts towards his wife.

- **Psychological aggression**, which includes threats, humiliations, frequent and unjustified repression, violence towards belongings or pets in order to intimidate, and trying to control the victim's access to money and friends. This may occur equally among women and men.

Although physical and psychological violence are different, the aim is one and the

same: To limit the victim's freedom or force him/her to do something they do not want to.

Social sectors at greater risk of violence

Violence within the couple appears in all social classes, nationalities, cultures and age-groups. However, certain sectors show a greater incidence:

- **Young people**. Age and domestic violence are statistically linked. In young couples (below the age of thirty), the incidence is double to that found in the over thirty age-group (Gelles, R.J., 1997).

- **Unemployed or low income sectors**. Lack of financial resources is also related to abusive behavior. As in the previous case, the probability of it occurring is doubled in low income families (Steinmetz, S.K., 1987).

- **Individual sectors with low levels of academic qualification**. Lack of education and academic background are also risk factors. Although violence does exist among well-educated people, it is more frequent among those who are unqualified.

- **Those who consume alcohol**. A high proportion of violent acts toward a partner are due to alcoholic drinks. A drinker, even when not drunk, loses his/her inhibitions and gives a free rein to aggressive behavior which probably would not happen in the absence of alcohol (Gelles, R.J., 1997).

In most cases, abuse within the couple follows a pattern characterized by three phases:

1. **A rise in tension**
2. **Violence**
3. **Promises**

Tension usually rises in situations of conflict, stress or negative emotions. When the aggressor reaches a high pressure point, he loses control and perpetrates the aggression. After this aggression he (or she) feels guilty and wants to avoid future incidents, promising to change and treating the victim with special affection and tact and even making concessions and giving valuable gifts. This exerts a reinforcing effect on the victim who stays in the relationship only because of this third phase.

• **Those who come from a violent family**. Being brought up in a violent family is another risk factor for reproducing this behavior. And this is true both for the aggressor and for the victim. A boy observes and learns the role from the father; violent, impatient, dominant behavior which in turn he will tend to reproduce. A girl observes her mother's role; a victim who suffers, humiliated, attitudes which facilitate abusive behavior (Kruttschnitt, C., Heath, L. and Ward, D.A., 1986).

Personality factors under greatest risk

There are certain personality attributes which also increase the risk of violence with-in the couple:

• **Lack of self-esteem.** **Self-esteem** is a factor associated with violence, both in the perpetrator and in the victim. The former feels inferior and wishes to compensate for his inferiority by displaying violence and toughness. The latter adopts a passive, suffering role, accepting she is worth little or that she is very miserable and does not deserve better treatment.

• **Jealousy**. It is often seen that those who suffer from unfounded jealousy, are at risk of displaying aggressive behavior, to try to prove by force what they have been unable to prove with reason.

• **Lack of assertiveness**. Those who beat their wives are usually endowed with few communication skills and little assertiveness. They find it difficult to express their point of view or reveal their desires in the correct way, through dialog and persuasion. Therefore they end up resorting to coercive methods.

• **The tendency to blame**. Blaming others, especially a partner, is also a common feature in those who display violence in their relationship. They feed on dispensing due "punishment" to the victim who is the cause of their misfortune.

Finally there are reasons of a cultural and social nature which contribute to the display and support of this evil. A highly competitive society, messages from the mass media with aggressive models, competitive sports, the woman presented as an object, etc. are all causes, which at least in part, serve to foster aggressive behavior.

The consequences of violence within a couple are tremendous. Firstly we have the typical physical injuries: marks from blows, burns, broken bones, cuts and so on. How-ever, this is not the only evidence; rather they are accompanied by other symptoms: insomnia, fretfulness, chronic headaches and backaches. In the last instance victims end up with serious mental disorders: Depression, anxiety, post-traumatic stress, low self-esteem, suicide, or murder at the hands of their partner.

When there are children, the consequences extend to them. Some of the childhood problems arising from this type of family situation are: Behavioral problems, difficulties at school, lying, theft, depression, anxiety and the notorious risk of becoming a victim or aggressor in adulthood.

Types of intervention in the face of violence

There are three basic intervention modes:

- **Legal**. The perpetrator is reported to the authorities that proceed with his arrest and prosecution. The victim requires adequate legal advice to follow the most suitable procedure in each case.

- **Social**. To remove the danger to which an abused woman is exposed, there are hostels sponsored by local authorities, non-governmental organizations or churches to help women and their children both in the practical issues (protection, housing, meals etc.), as well as providing the emotional support so necessary during this time.

- **Psychotherapeutic**. Those who work closely with these cases state that changes in behavior are rare and it is necessary to concentrate on protecting the victim. However, some cases, where there is the will to improve, do respond well to psychotherapy. The intervention is the same as that described for cases of jealousy (see the previous section). The aggressor is helped to dominate his thoughts, desires and behavior and he is taught techniques to solve his problems creatively and effectively. The victim is trained how to improve her self-concept, to think more rationally and to free herself of her feelings of guilt.

Due to stressful experiences, family conflict, or simply the passage of time, one member (or both) in a couple may suffer problems in their sex life. The immense majority of sexual dis-orders are resolved between the couple themselves. Dialog, communication, affection and tenderness are often enough to return to a balanced situation.

However, at other times problems become so complex that they go beyond the reach of dialog and mutual understanding and require advice or treatment from a sex therapist or medical specialist.

Sometimes a couple hears or reads remarks which make them think that their sex life is unsatisfactory. This is common due to the media that often portrays sexual behavior in an exaggerated or fantasized manner. A couple should remember that in order to talk of a dysfunction or disorder, the problem should produce:

• A significant level of stress and
• Serious difficulties in the marital relationship.

In the absence of these criteria, one cannot diagnose the disorders covered in the box on the following page. If, for example, an apparent premature ejaculation does not prove to be a source of stress or conflict within the couple and both feel sexually satisfied, we cannot talk of a sexual dysfunction.

Therapy applied to sexual dysfunctions is highly effective. In their years of practice, Masters and Johnson, for example, achieved a cure rate of 84% among treated males and 78% in women (Alpern, D.M., 1988).

Therapy has the advantage that even when a perfect solution is not achieved, there is always great improvement. The biggest problem occurs when those who suffer such disorders are reticent about going to see a sex therapist or medical specialist.

What does this therapy consist of? The basis of sexual therapy is education. The therapist listens to the couple's problems and provides information. The couples learn about the physiology related to their sexual relations, they are instructed in techniques for relaxation, they acquire the habit of talking about sexually-related matters, they learn to explore their partner's body and so on. The partners also clarify their attitudes toward their own bodies, their partner's body and their sexual relations. This information, together with the right attitude, is enough to correct their problems.

If being well-informed and possessing a change of attitude prove insufficient, they are taught **specific sexual techniques**, according to the dysfunction they are dealing with. For example, there are techniques to control ejaculation or to relax the cervical muscles and thus avoid vaginismus. The therapist explains the technique, the patient tries the technique privately at home with his or her partner, and then both return to the doctor's practice to report on the results.

When problems of a physiological etiology exist, pharmacological treatment under medical supervision is indicated.

The most complicated cases are related to events from the past which have produced some kind of psychological trauma that seriously impedes sexual functions. In these cases it would not be convenient to proceed with any technique without first submitting the patient to extensive psychotherapy in order to reach the root of the problem. These are the rarest cases as represented in the pyramid graph to our left.

Deep Therapy

Training in Techniques

Sex Education

The most widely-used classification currently employed, divides sexual dysfunctions within the couple into four types, according to whether they appear in the sexual desire phase, during arousal, during orgasm or if intercourse is painful (taken from the most accredited international diagnostic system, DSM-IV-R).

1. Sexual desire disorders

Hypoactive sexual desire. This is the absence or marked deficiency of desires to maintain sexual relations. Although in some cases this may be attributed to medical problems (hormone or metabolic alterations, medicines …) the most frequent causes are emotional in nature: psychological tension or states of depression.

Sexual Aversion. This is the rejection and avoidance of sexual contact while experiencing anxiety, fear or disgust regarding sex. This is usually rooted in traumatic events from the past (having received a strict, puritan upbringing or having been sexually abused as a child).

2. Sexual arousal disorders

Female arousal. This is the difficulty in achieving or maintaining vaginal lubrication and engorgement which accompany sexual arousal. This leads to pain during intercourse which is then avoided. The causes are of a psycho-emotional nature.

Male erectile disorder (impotence). This consists of difficulties in achieving or maintaining an erection until the end of the sex act. This produces dissatisfaction for the woman and feelings of frustration and failure in the man. The cause is sometimes physiological but anxiety and fear of failure are always present. This problem tends to increase in middle age.

3. Orgasmic disorders

Female orgasmic disorder. The woman experiences a normal arousal phase but this does not culminate in orgasm or it is excessively delayed.

Male orgasmic disorder. The man experiences a normal arousal phase but this does not culminate in orgasm or it is excessively delayed. Those suffering this disorder describe normal arousal and penetration; however the activity of intercourse becomes tiresome instead of pleasurable.

Premature ejaculation. The man experiences ejaculation with a minimum of sexual stimulation prior to penetration or directly afterwards. This leads to his partner's dissatisfaction and feelings of failure in the man.

4. Sexual disorders due to pain

Dyspareunia. This disorder consists of genital pain during the sex act. This pain may become very intense. It is a rare disorder, the causes of which are of a psychological nature.

Vaginismus. This occurs when a woman experiences involuntary muscular spasms which hinder intercourse and produce sexual dissatisfaction in both spouses. The problem appears most frequently among women with a negative attitude towards sex or in those who have suffered some kind of trauma or sexual abuse.

Household arguments and bickering seem small when compared with a true crisis situation for a couple or a family. We are referring to events such as the **sudden loss of employment**, divorce or a **traumatic accident or the death** of a family member.

Components of a crisis

A crisis happens as the result of a crucial change in the normal course of family events. Every crisis has at least three components:

- Significant change.
- Lack of stability.
- The opportunity to make decisions (positive and negative).

In couples and families, these situations are comparable to a vessel that capsizes. Some important atmospheric change places the boat in a dangerous, unstable situation thus forcing the crew to make important decisions. These may be positive (employment of advanced emergency means and methods to save the situation) or negative (loss of control and desperation).

Stages in a crisis

In general, crises follow a set route, passing through the following stages:

1. **The advent of the crisis**. The events producing a family crisis come about in an atmosphere of great tension (or stress). For example, a heart attack in a father of fifty. The crisis may be set off by a situation of extreme stress or by the accumulation of several smaller stressful circumstances which produce an overload.

2. **A period of disorganization**. The sudden load causes a severe blow to the family. The heart attack takes his wife and children by surprise. A short while after the initial shock, they have to make arrangements to help the father, speak to the doctors, change schedules etc. It is a difficult time in which no sense can be made of this misfortune, they think about how it might have been avoided, who is to blame … In these circumstances the family requires more emotional and practical support from friends, relatives and professionals.

3. **A period of reorganization and recuperation**. After touching bottom, the problem starts on the road to recovery. When the ill person is out of danger, he is told to rest for several weeks. This is a variation in the family's normal life, but a way can be found to overcome this: Systematic help from members of the family, support and instruction for the patient, or social workers who help him to take on a lifestyle which will prevent a relapse, and so on.

4. **A period of stabilization**. This involves a return to normality, although under certain circumstances it will not be the same as before the crisis. In our example the patient resumes his normal working life and everyone enters a stable situation after the troubles.

Many people
are subject to an
unexpected critical
experience and do
not have time to react
appropriately. It is very
useful to understand
how one should face a crisis, by familiarizing
oneself with certain basic steps to deal with it in
a satisfactory fashion. The fundamental questions
are: **How should a crisis be faced? What measures
should be taken to safely resolve this situation?**

Divorce is a growing problem. Only in countries where it is legally restricted is it under control. But why do people get divorced? The explanations offered by divorcees to lawyers or judges could well be stereotypical, convenient answers to avoid drawing the process out any longer than is necessary. The real causes perhaps remain hidden or are confided only to the closest family or friends. One of the most reliable sources are the psychotherapists who help one or other partner to overcome the crisis.

Causes of divorce

Data gathered by a group of psychotherapists for the couple (see Whisman, M.A., Dixon, A.E. and Johnson, B., 1998) show the following reasons for divorce as presented by their patients in descending order of frequency:

1. **Communication problems** ("We don't understand each other.")
2. **Problems of authority** ("We can't reach agreements. Both of us want to be in control.")
3. **Unrealistic expectations** ("Marriage should be some-thing marvelous.")
4. **Sexuality** ("I'm not satisfied with our sex life.")

Other reasons are: Absence of loving feelings, conflicts of values, personality problems, marital infidelity, lack of affection and money issues. Furthermore, there are reasons which, while less frequent (if compared with the total number of divorces), are nonetheless highly significant: Abuse toward a spouse, abuse towards children, homosexuality, alcohol and other drugs.

Reasons of a sociological nature

There are also reasons of a sociological nature which explain divorce according to temporal and geographical variations:

1. **The legal context**. Countries with laws which facilitate divorce display higher indices than those which place many legal obstacles before people who wish to get divorced.

2. **The feminist movement**. Women have correctly grown to understand that being a wife is not a synonym for slavery, and many women with dysfunctional marriages have taken the necessary steps to get a divorce.

3. **Economic development**. The most opulent regions of the world show the highest rate of divorce. Divorce requires economic means or possibilities for surviving after the break-up, especially for women, who in many countries are denied such financial self-sufficiency.

Continued on page 94

The findings of a study at the University of Harvard (McLanahan, S. and Sandefur, G., 1994) maintain that all the members of a family suffering from a high level of conflict, for example where there is persistent abuse or alcoholism, benefit from divorce. However, those marriages with a low level of conflict gain more by staying together, and the harm to the children is less than that caused by divorce. With this, we are expressing the view that although couples, amidst certain disagreements, see divorce as a viable solution, they should endeavor to find a solution to their problems and thus prevent a divorce.

Below we have outlined a group of strategies aimed at preventing divorce:

- *Resolution of conflicts.* To overcome the array of conflicts which necessarily arise out of living together, it is necessary to be well prepared in conflict resolution skills.

- *Constant verbal exchange.* A lack of verbal exchange and effective communication is a very subtle, pernicious problem in married life. Regular conversation, from the most inconsequential to the most intimate, is imperative. This activity strengthens trust, friendship and loving bonds.

- *Share authority and duties.* An authoritarian attitude on the part of one or both of the spouses may trigger a crisis. In a relationship founded on love, the greater part of one's happiness is found in making a loved one happy. It is therefore necessary to share the different duties incumbent in living as a couple or a family and reaching agreements which please both partners concerning the distribution of these responsibilities.

- *Do not think of marriage as a fairy tale.* Spouses should never expect a perfect relationship which fully satisfies them in all aspects. If they think like this, their disappointment and dissatisfaction will be such that they will want to separate. Both have to think that a happy marriage is only achieved with a good measure of endeavor and sacrifice on both parts. And even with good will on both parts, the relationship will go through some frustrating moments.

- *Keep your sex life alive.* Sexual dissatisfaction, as we have already mentioned, may be one reason for seeking other options which may destroy a marriage. This aspect should not be neglected at any time during a relationship.

- *Loving and romantic feelings.* A relationship full of romantic touches and loving words and gestures is fundamental for keeping the flame of love alight. This is of special significance to women. It is therefore of utmost importance not to fall into a routine of not expressing love for each other.

Of course, one way of preventing divorce is by not to enter a high-risk marriage relationship with very high chances of failure. The box "Bad reasons for getting married", on page 25 gives examples of such problems, although there is always the possibility of saving a difficult marriage.

Continued from page 92

4. **Lifestyle**. The stressful environment prevalent today fosters impatience, hostility and intolerance. If such traits are brought into a couple's life together, this is made even more difficult. It is then that divorce is considered an option.

5. **The divorce culture**. Independently of their level of development, there are countries which possess a divorce culture. In such places, divorce has a long tradition and has been common for many years and among all social classes. As such, the steps to be undertaken are well defined and integrated into normal everyday life.

6. **Social approval**. It is increasingly more frequent to come across couples in which the partners have been previously married, with children who live with siblings of different parents, and parents-in-law with two sons and four daughters-in-law. This incidence of divorce means that there is less social stigma attached to it, thus making the road of divorce more bearable.

7. **The absence of a religious influence**. As was seen in the first chapter, marriage is a divine invention, sacred in nature and integrated into human existence from its very beginnings. When people expel religious meaning from their lives, they also do so from their marriages. Marriage thus becomes a contract between two individuals (without divine authority). The contract may be rescinded when both parties deem it appropriate, a very different concept to a religious marriage which is only dissolved under extreme and highly specific circumstances.

Many couples when going through problems consider divorce as an escape route. But divorce is not an easy road. In fact, a divorce process may be one of the most traumatic experiences of one's life. It is therefore necessary to try every available means to avoid divorce and achieve satisfaction.

In every couple's relationship there always has to be room for forgiveness, a highly gratifying experience both for the person granting and the person receiving it. When one spouse deeply hurts the other, a significant disturbance is produced in the relationship. And in these cases it is necessary to restore balance. If this does not happen then one runs the risk of wearing down or shattering the relationship. Forgiveness is the appropriate way of returning a marital relationship to good health.

Dr. *Mario Pereyra*, proposes the following four stages of forgiveness. These phases clearly show the therapeutic power of forgiveness when accompanied by understanding on the part of both spouses.

1. *Making oneself morally conscious*. To start the process of forgiveness, the offender has to recognize his or her offending attitude or behavior. In psychological terms this is referred to as insight or sudden inner awakening to the moral mistake made. For example, a husband who has been unfaithful to his wife cannot enjoy her forgiveness unless he is fully convinced of the immorality of his conduct. Without taking this initial step he will be unable to begin any rehabilitating experience.

2. *Decision*. Once in a state of moral awareness, the individual may choose from several alternative ways out of his/ her situation. It is a crossroads: "I have hurt and I am truly repentant. What should I do? Should I confess and ask for forgiveness, or cover up the offence and live alone with my guilt?" The first option is the healthiest as the second leads to serious mental health problems, apart from a progressive deterioration in the relationship.

3. *Asking for forgiveness*. Steps 1 and 2 are full of internal tension, private turmoil within the offender's conscience. But once the decision in favor of forgiveness and reconciliation is taken, then comes action: To explicitly confess, ask for forgiveness, acknowledge one's mistake, all face to face. When this is a genuine act, it tends to promote a magnanimous reaction in the spouse, making it easier for him or her to grant forgiveness.

4. *Beyond forgiveness*. After receiving forgiveness the offender needs to repair the damage done, i.e. do everything in his/her power to bring about a full restoration. Furthermore, forgiveness involves a real "forgetting" of the past, on the part of the aggrieved party together with the firm resolution by the offender not to recur in the mistake.

This process contains deeply healing powers; through its use a relationship may reach even greater levels of complicity and happiness than those of its beginnings. However, it is necessary to be warned that often, and especially in cases of constant abuse or reiterated adultery, the process may not work. Indeed, there is often an apparent repentance (simple fruit of remorse), but once forgiveness is secured the situation recurs, entering into a vicious circle from which it becomes more and more difficult to escape. There would seem to be no sense in forgiveness here as it does not lead to positive results.

Differences and how to live with them

One of the causes of marital confrontation and breakup, is the total lack of knowledge concerning the existing differences between men and women. The boxes on this page and on the following one give an overview of these differences, both from the biological and psychological viewpoints. The differences inherent in both sexes, when well understood and accepted, may serve to complement the deficiencies incumbent on both sides. The couple can thus come to form a more consolidated and complete entity.

The physical differences are undeniable and affect both a man's and a woman's behavior. Their psychological differences may be derived from their culture, the effect of socialization and the environment in general. But whatever their origin, differences do exist and they should be used in the most beneficial way.

Getting to know these differences well is fundamental if the couple hopes to reduce the likelihood of divorce and achieve a successful relationship together. It is strange that to drive a car or build an electrical installation one needs a license which certifies due preparation. However to embark on a marriage (which is where habits, thoughts and behaviors are taught and where children and young people are educated for the rest of their lives) not even a week-long course is required.

Candidates for marriage ought to have to take an examination on the basic lessons of matrimonial life . One of those lessons should concern the differences between men and women and how to live with them. Herein we have outlined some of the most important points in this fundamental lesson:

- **Women need to talk**. An immense majority of women require large doses of conversation to

PSYCHOLOGICAL DIFFERENCES

Women

1. Oriented towards people, with greater possibilities of establishing optimal interpersonal relationships.
2. Predominantly verbal. They face problems by talking them through and in arguments they rarely come to blows.
3. Predominantly emotional.
4. They possess keen intuition.
5. They project their emotions and their own identity onto the task they are undertaking. This explains why women are usually more passionate about what they do.
6. They are interested in personal and human details, and in anecdotes and stories.

Men

1. Oriented towards practical issues, duties, obligations and objects rather than people.
2. Predominantly physical. They face problems through action and in arguments they may come to blows.
3. Eminently practical.
4. Their intuition is weaker in favor of logic.
5. They maintain their identity outside their work. This explains why men carry out their duties in an intense, yet objective way.
6. They are interested in facts and data, rather than in personal issues or details.

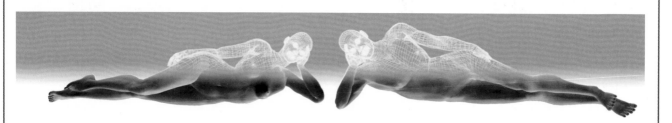

Women

1. Their constitution allows them to live longer.
2. Their metabolism is slower than a man's.
3. Their overall bone structure is different to a man's. It is less around the face and legs and greater in the trunk.
4. They have certain organs which are larger than a man's (kidneys, liver, stomach, appendix and thyroid gland).
5. They have certain exclusive bodily functions: menstruation, gestation and lactation.
6. Their blood has a higher water content and 20% fewer red blood cells.
7. Their muscles account for 23% of their body mass
8. Their average pulse rate is 80 per minute.
9. They show greater resistance to high temperatures than men do.

Men

1. On average men live six or seven years less than women.
2. Their metabolism is faster than a woman's.
3. They have a greater bone formation around the head, their chins are more prominent and their faces are thinner.
4. A man's lungs are on average larger than a woman's.
5. Their hormone system is different and this means they lack the physiological functions found in women.
6. The composition of their blood is different to a woman's as it has less water and more red blood cells.
7. Their muscles account for up to 40% of their body mass.
8. Their average pulse rate is 72 per minute.
9. Their metabolism limits their threshold to high temperature resistance.

maintain their emotional integrity. Women need to talk and they need someone to listen to them with genuine interest and affection. They need to talk about endless details, people and topics. It is part of the female psychology. Many women satisfy this need through a girlfriend or neighbor; but their marriages would run more smoothly if their husbands were willing to fulfill this listening role.

- **Men need to do things**. While women solve problems by talking through them, men provide solutions by keeping their mouths closed and taking action. This may be seen at home when they mend a tap, repair the car, drill holes in walls and so on. It is also seen in games, sports and entertainment: Playing football or tennis, fishing etc. It is about "doing things". And a woman has to understand this need, as well. The ideal situation is that a wife is her husband's companion in such activities. But even if she does not like any of her husband's pastimes, she should at least give him the necessary leeway to enable him to practice some of his pastimes with his friends.

- **Female hormones create special needs in a woman**. Women are subject to a fairly predictable menstrual cycle which produces certain specific characteristics during the days leading up to the beginning of their period. Some women, between 8 and 10%, experience such acute hormonal changes that they suffer "premenstrual syndrome" [Wurtman, R.J and Wurtman, J.J., *Scientific American*, 260 (1)]. However, all women, are affected in some way to a greater or lesser extent: Mood swings, anxiety, irritability, headaches, backache, dizziness or constipation (American Council on Science and Health, 1985). Their partners need to be alert for these days in order to be especially tolerant, treating them attentively and with affection and being willing to support them.

- **Male hormones make a man especially driven towards sex**. A man is subject to a much stronger and more frequent sex drive than a woman. Any small stimulus arouses his sexual appetite and he is swiftly willing to satisfy it. In a context of dialog and mutual respect, a woman should understand these hormonal and affective needs and help her partner to satisfy them.

- **A woman is oriented toward her family and friends**. Female socialization centers especially around her family and to a lesser degree her friends. It is therefore frequent to see a wife organize a visit to her parents, her brothers and sisters or her friends or work colleagues (or she invites them to her house). There are men who look on this with indifference and others who are bothered by it. It is, in any case, a social need more emphasized among women, and men should, as far as possible, give it their backing and respect.

- **Men are oriented to their working circles**. For most men their trade or profession is of prime importance and they devote a good part of their energy to this area. This commitment is linked to supporting their family in its material and economic needs. A man sets great store by this. His wife, therefore, needs to

understand this strong male tendency of adopting the breadwinning role and to approve of this attitude, as long as it is not taken to extremes and becomes a risk to his health.

As in everything, these generalizations will vary in couples with partners who are extreme opposites or show different needs. In such cases they would have to reach the necessary understanding to resolve their particular problems. The main thing is to be aware of those differences and to do everything possible to understand and attend to those characteristics in order to build a satisfying marriage and prevent divorce.

There are no exceptions, in age or circumstances, when children do not suffer bitterly in the process of divorce. Over the last few decades there has been a build-up in psychological and sociological research aimed at identifying the wounds and scars a divorce leaves on youngsters. Findings are divided between:

- Studies stating that divorce leaves permanent marks which accompany them into adulthood (Wallerstein, J. S. and Blakeslee, S., 1996).

- Studies confirming that divorce seriously affects young children for a limited period (generally the first two years following the separation), but they can return to normal after that (Buchanan, C.M., Maccoby, E.E. and Dornbusch, S.M., 1996).

But all studies found that the divorce process affects the children's normal development in some way. All children went through a *painful experience*.

The effect is largely dependent on the childhood problems present prior to the divorce. Those children already in a problematic situation tend to suffer in the extreme. On the other hand, those who did not have problems before the divorce, are quicker in returning to normal.

The adverse effects of divorce on children

Below we have listed some of the adverse effects that a divorce may have on children:

- **Emotional imbalance**, shown through tears, irritability or undefined worries.

- **Undesirable behavior**, such as aggression towards siblings or other children, or distancing themselves socially, isolation.

- **Symptoms of depression**: lack of appetite, sleep disturbances, especially awaking with a start in the middle of the night.

- **Problems at school**: Sharp falls in academic achievement and behavioral problems at school.

- **In the long term**, children belonging to divorced families tend to experience more problems in their courting and marital relationships.

Sufficient support should always be made available to children to enable them to face these difficult moments. Their parents, usually a child's main source of emotional comfort, are, at this time, totally affected by the divorce. Therefore, during this transition period, the role of teachers, grandparents or family friends and relatives may prove highly valuable in occupying the children in positive jobs and conversations which help them to overcome their parents' divorce with the least possible suffering. The greater the number of arguments there are between the parents, the more **psychological problems** appear in the children.

The risk becomes even higher when children witness fights or are the topic of a quarrel (for example concerning visiting rights or payment of a child's expenses). If such wrangling is not avoided, for however much we may want to keep the children or youngsters out of these experiences, they **will feel involved** in the conflict. Sometimes a thorny topic needs to be discussed. In these cases the discussion should be carried out in private, or out of the children's earshot. It is better to use a public venue such as a park or a café where a calm conversation may be held.

In many countries divorce is on the rise. This means that there are increasingly more youngsters affected by such an event. For many, divorce puts them in a worse situation than before. For others, victims of violence and abuse, divorce comes as a relief. But in every case, getting back to normality will be a long and difficult road, on occasions leaving long-lasting scars.

It is the parents who need to make a greater effort to help their children pass through this critical moment with the least possible risk. Their action should be aimed in two directions: firstly, towards their children, offering them valid explanations and messages of affection; and secondly towards their ex-spouse, dealing with him or her in such a way that the children are free of any adverse effects derived from possible disputes.

How to explain a divorce to them

The explanations given will have to be adapted to the child's age:

- **Children under the age** of two do not understand nor need to understand what divorce means, but they are affected by the changes in routine that it implies. There-fore, the best way of dealing with the very young is keeping scrupulously to their routines in regards to times for sleeping, eating, playing and so on.

- **The kindergarten age group** (3 to 6-year-olds) do have a certain capacity for understanding what the absence or presence of one of their parents means. For this reason, trying to pretend and acting as if nothing had changed is useless and even counterproductive. For the good of the children certain questions and concerns have to be addressed briefly yet honestly: "Who am I going to be with?" "Where will my toys be?" "Does daddy still love me?" "Does mummy still love me?" "Are they going to leave me on my own?"

- **School-age children** (6 to 12-year-olds) need fuller answers without going into detail. They want to know things concerning their routines: Timetables, the days they can see their father (or mother), if their parents are going to get back together again. One aspect of utmost importance is the risk of them feeling guilty or responsible for the divorce. Many children believe they are the cause of their parents' separation. They need to hear clearly from both parents that this matter is due to problems between mom and dad and that they are not to blame at all. They also have to be taught how to answer the questions their friends and class-mates may ask them, because what other people think begins to be important to them at this age.

- **Adolescents** (13 to 18-year-olds) may be considerably affected by their parents' divorce. Some may attempt suicide or engage in antisocial behavior. Adolescents tend to display anger towards their parents and themselves. This has to be accepted and patience should be shown towards them. Some feel guilty. As they are capable of understanding, they deserve to know why their parents are getting divorced, but again without going into detail.

- **At all levels** it is important to be ethical, not to deceive, to try to make the children feel loved and accepted by both parents. A hurt spouse will often use his/her children as a shoulder to cry on, but before doing this he/she should think: What is best for the child?

To be able to pass through all these difficulties and come out unscathed, support is required from more or less qualified professionals. Be it through a number of psychotherapy sessions, or through the support of a confidante (friend or relative) or by attending a self-help group which brings together people who have undergone a similar experience, the divorcee needs to be in contact with people who offer an optimal social atmosphere where he/she feels warmth and acceptance. In any case, the passage of time is a decisive factor in getting over a divorce.

Being overly friendly is out of place. However hostility is not appropriate either as it is hurtful to everyone. The best relationship between former spouses is one which is **distant, polite and devoid of sentiment;** something like a business relationship.

Even when great pains are taken, there are times when some matter concerning the children or the divorce agreement cannot be resolved by mutual agreement. In extreme cases an impartial mediator should be employed (a friend of both former spouses or a psychotherapist), to arbitrate in the situation and suggest reasonable agreements for both parties.

Living without bearing a grudge

For decades it was thought that repressing anger was dangerous for one's sanity. This is no longer considered valid. Today it is held that:

- Accumulated **grudges**, or their close relative, **wrath**, produce more **strain and destruction** than any other emotion.

- *Getting angry is not good for one's emotional well-being*. Harboring grudges will only serve to prejudice one's health and happiness.

- *Grudges are not created by others, but are made within oneself*. Although other people may contribute to their development, grudges are

the product of our own thoughts and attitudes. This negative emotion has to be **channeled** so that it does not cause us harm.

- Not holding a grudge leads to a deep feeling of **respect** from the other party.

The solution is not easy, but perhaps it would be useful to reflect on the words of Albert Einstein: *"Peace cannot be achieved through violence, it can only be attained through understanding."*

We are not being asked to pass from hostility to love. But what we did say at the beginning of this chapter was that it is desirable that a relationship between former spouses be **respectful**, polite and **distant**; summing up, **peace free from grudges** with a state of mind which wishes a former spouse all the best from the bottom of one's heart, because we should still aspire to being happy.

In old age

Chapter Summary

*E*dward and Martha got married forty years ago and now they are about to enter their retirement period together. They have three married children and five grandchildren. Behind them are various jobs, several homes, moments of anxiety, of uncertainty, of health crises and a host of pleasant memories, full of happiness. The overall balance is positive. They are happy about the road they have traveled together. They also rejoice in having reached retirement in optimum conditions.

They already have concrete plans. He, in his profession as an accountant, never had enough time for what he wanted to do—cabinetwork. And furthermore, he will read much more. Martha, who until now has been a shop assistant in a department store, is going to make new curtains for her own and her children's homes, and she also has other projects … They will go out for walks in the afternoons and they will visit relatives and friends from time to time.

In these times of marital and family crises, reaching retirement age together as a happily married couple can be considered an achievement, as is successfully confronting the stage of retirement.

There are countries and cultures where grandparents play only a minimal role in the care of their grandchildren. The traditional role, where grandmother looked after her grandchildren while her daughter went to work, is disappearing little by little. However, in many other contexts, grandparents (due to their living nearby and having more free time than parents) play a primary role in the upbringing of their grandchildren.

The most common activities grandparents carry out with their grandchildren include playing with them, telling them stories, taking them for walks, talking and joking with them, preparing meals for them, giving them pocket money and watching television with them … The continued company of many grandparents with their grandchildren identifies them as an important means of transmitting values. For this reason grandparents should think that they are partly responsible for forming their grandchildren's characters.

The traditional positions on intellectual development explained that intelligence decreased with age. Today, it is understood that intellectual abilities decrease only in specific areas, namely symbolic knowledge and speed of reaction. In fact, it has been found that at retirement age, one is wiser (a wider-reaching concept than intelligence) than in one's youth. This quality refers to real-life problem-solving in an effective and balanced way. This is the maturity which comes with years and why one should not disregard grandparents' and great-grandparents' advice.

Besides the transmitting and educating role of grandparents with their grandchildren, this role brings other benefits:

- Firstly, many grandparents feel transformed by their interaction with their grandchildren. In the words of a grandmother who had recently become widowed: "My granddaughter is my therapy."
- Secondly, the advent of grandchildren and great-grandchildren implies the survival of the grandparents' lineage, and this helps them to assimilate the idea of their own death.
- Lastly, when grandparents help in the upbringing of their grandchildren and they are with them for periods of time, they transfer to them their own childhood experiences, thus accepting their past in a resolved way. This again helps them to calmly contemplate their final days.

A couple's capacity for enjoying their sex life together continues in retirement to an advanced age.

The very most important factor for full and complete sexuality resides precisely in **keeping sexually active**. When an elderly couple cuts off their sexual relations for a prolonged period of time it is difficult to start them agin. On the other hand, couples who regularly maintain sexual relations, may continue to have intercourse beyond the age of 80.

The frequency of sexual activity decreases with age. According to several reports, 3 out of every 4 couples over 74 years of age claim to make love at least once a month; and 1 out of every 4 couples in the same age group, once a week (Fisher, L., 1999). Even when older people's sexual activity is less frequent, the encounters can be as pleasurable as in the past.

We provide some helpful information to enhance sexual activity for elderly people in the box "What to do to improve one's sexuality" on the following page.

This box lists the findings of different research projects regarding changes in sexuality at a mature age (Bremner, W.J., Vitiello, M.V., & Prinz, P.N., 1983; National Institute on Aging [NIA], 1980). Such variations do not necessarily imply the ceasing of sexual activity, but rather a continuation within the constraints imposed by one's physiology and a correct attitude. As long as both partners obtain physiological and emotional benefits from sexual activity, it should continue.

Variations	What to do
• Men take longer to reach an erection.	• Extend the period prior to intercourse or ejaculation, learning to enjoy further the intimacy of this mutual closeness.
• Men take longer to ejaculate.	• Use caresses and manual stimulation of the penis more so than in the past.
• Women experience the signs of arousal (increase in the size of breasts and clitoris) with less intensity.	• Accept this as a fact which should not hinder sexual enjoyment on either part.
• Women do not secrete sufficient vaginal fluid and the vaginal walls lose their flexibility.	• Use lubricant creams.
• A correct attitude fosters a more satisfying experience.	• Both husband and wife should consider sexuality in old age as something positive, beautiful and gratifying, despite what others may think.

Most accidents among the elderly take place in the kitchen, the bathroom and the bedroom. Falls are the most common events, followed by burns. Much of the advice offered here is simple, yet can avoid many tragedies.

In the kitchen ...

- Keep the utensils and saucepans you often use **within reach**.
- When you need to reach a high object, use a steady stool with a step if you do not have a safe **step-ladder** available.
- If a liquid is spilt on the floor, **mop it up** immediately. You may easily forget it and slip.
- Use **rubber-soled** slippers to avoid falls-.
- Use **short sleeves** or tight cuffs to prevent your clothes from catching fire.
- Get used to cooking on a **low heat**. It is healthier and reduces the risk of fire.
- Keep tea-towels, curtains and other flammable cloth items **away from** heat sources.
- Keep work-tops **free** of objects and food. There always should be room to place a boiling saucepan.

- Use a timer **with an alarm** to remind you that something is cooking.
- If you use gas, make sure that the installation and **servicing** are done by qualified personnel.
- When you leave the kitchen, take a **last look** to ensure that everything is switched off and all the plugs are out.

In the bathroom ...

- Place a **rubber mat** in the bath or shower basin, or use any other technical means to avoid slipping.
- Install one or more **handrails** on the walls of the shower or bath. There are also systems whereby you can take showers **sitting down**.
- **Avoid moveable throw** rugs which may slide or cause you to trip. If you want to lay carpet, do so from wall to wall with a permanent fitting system.

- **Do not lock the bathroom door**. You may need urgent help at some time.
- When you take a bath, ensure the water is not **too hot**. First run the cold water and then add the hot until the water reaches the temperature you want.
- In the shower, **mix the water** carefully and in any case do not set the water-heater at a very high temperature.
- If you notice that a plug gives off sparks, **have it repaired** immediately. The bathroom is a high-risk area for electrocution.

In the bedroom ...
- Keep a small bedside lamp or light switch **close at hand**. Getting up in the dark is an unnecessary risk.
- The bed should be at the **correct height**. When seated on the bed, the soles of your feet should touch the ground. Beds which are either too high or too low present possible risk.

- Some older people experience dizziness when getting out of bed. This can be avoided by first **sitting on** the bed for a few moments before carefully getting to one's feet.
- The cords for lamps, telephones, etc. should run **around the walls** and never across the middle of a room or under a rug.
- Keep heat sources **away from** curtains, bed-spreads, etc, to avoid the risk of fire.
- Never smoke in bed. Fires caused by this habit have taken many lives. In any case, it is better **not to smoke** at all; your body will thank you for it.
- Avoid using electric blankets and pillows. If you do use them, **switch them off** before going to sleep.
- Keep **a telephone close to your bed**. Many emergency calls are made from the bedroom and this precautionary measure may save your life.

Enrich your partner's self-esteem

- **Observe and study your spouse**. After so many years of living together, there are things which go unseen because they are taken for granted. Observe his/her tasks, the way he/she addresses others, his/her way of smiling, the solutions he/she gives to problems, his/her sense of humor; in summary, everything which makes up your partner's rich personality.

- **Take note of the most worthy aspects**. After affectionately observing your partner, make a mental note of the things you most appreciate in him or her.

- **Verbally communicate those aspects which please you**. Speak openly to your spouse about his/her virtues in a loving emotive tone. Communicate specific things:

  ✓ How delicious that meal was.

  ✓ Household tasks well done.

  ✓ How well he/she entertains the grandchildren.

  ✓ His/her sweet way of talking.

- **Do not joke about or ridicule your spouse**. You can hurt his/her self-esteem by doing this, especially in the presence of other people. A sensitive person will never take things as a joke but will feel more insecure.

- **Look after your own self-esteem**. It is often true that in order to nourish another person's self-esteem, one must have a good self concept. For this reason many psychologists work on building-up one spouse's self concept in order to ultimately help the other partner.

As the years go by we experience a certain deterioration of our organism. Although there are some people whose faculties remain intact until a very advanced age, a certain loss of faculties is considered normal among elderly people.

- A loss **in vision** is one of the natural processes associated with aging. Part of our visual problems can be corrected using glasses, contact lenses or ophthalmological operations. Others, such as **cataracts** (which affect 50% of retired people), require surgery. Whichever the case may be, these problems interfere with everyday tasks such as reading, sewing, or shopping. Elderly people, even if they use corrective lenses, should carefully avoid possible accidents. For example, it may be appropriate to avoid driving at night, or night-time activities.

- A loss in **keenness of hearing** is also related to old age. It is estimated that around 50% of all people over 60 experience hearing problems. And, of these, over half have a degree of hearing loss which significantly impedes their leading a normal life. Men suffer a greater loss of hearing than women. Do the

Can you hear properly?

1. When you turn up the volume on the radio and the television, do the rest of the family complain?
   ○ Yes ○ No

2. Do you often wonder why people do not speak louder and more clearly?
   ○ Yes ○ No

3. Does it often happen that you have to ask because you have not fully understood what people have said?
   ○ Yes ○ No

4. When you go to a public place which is noisy and full of people, do you have serious problems in understanding what is being said?
   ○ Yes ○ No

5. Is it true that the telephone or the doorbell sometimes rings and you do not hear it?
   ○ Yes ○ No

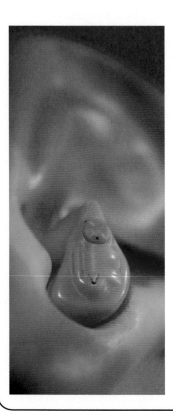

If you have answered "Yes" to one or more of these questions, go to see your doctor or a specialist to have a hearing test. The practitioner may recommend you buy a hearing aid. The loss of hearing has no cure, but a hearing aid, applied directly in the ear, amplifies certain high and low tones and will help you to hear better.

test "Can you hear properly?", which appears in the box on this page, and you will find out if you need to see a specialist.

- Our **sense of smell** becomes less acute, as does our sense of **taste**, which is dependent on the former. Women conserve both senses better than men. One of the problems derived from a decrease in one's sense of taste is that food has less flavor. A word of advice: As this loss is more pronounced in savory, bitter and sour flavors, but not in sweet ones, beware of abusing sweet or over-salted foods.

- **Strength, resistance, balance and speed** do all weaken with time. In spite of this, most jobs which are done earlier in life may still be carried out, if more slowly, during this stage in our lives.

- We know a builder who, at the age of 75, built a house entirely on his own. His explanation was: "I would have built this house in 6 to 8 months when I was younger, it has now taken me 2 years. The quality is the same, except now I do things more slowly."

The new line of geriatric research (Ades, P.A.; Ballor, D.L.; Ashikaga, T., Utton, J.L. and Nair, K.S., 1996. Fiatarone, M.A.; Marks, E.C.; Ryan, N.D.; Meredith, C.N.; Lipsitz, L.A. and Evans, W.J., 1990. Fiatarone, M.A.; O'Neill, E.F. y Ryan, N.D., 1994. McCartney, N.; Hicks, A.L.; Martin, J. y Webber, C.E., 1996) shows that motor loss during ageing can be recovered through appropriate exercises. It has been confirmed through motor training programs lasting between 2 and 24 months among participants aged 60 to 90, that important increases in muscle strength, size and mobility can be achieved. These findings are encouraging and assure us that our latter years can also be full of vitality and wellbeing.

- As far as the **general public health system for elderly peopl**e is concerned, today it is under pressure from two opposing forces. On the one hand, personal hygiene, water supply and sewage, the use of vaccines and antibiotics and the propagation of certain elementary principles in health care have prevented many diseases and premature deaths. Further-more, in developed countries, there is a long list of public services and equipment specifically for the comfort of elderly people.

However, we also find a series of diseases closely related to life-style. Several types of cancer, heart disease, strokes and high blood pressure are a sample of the many complications we suffer today due to a sedentary life-style, the use of tobacco and alcohol, an incorrect diet and a polluted environment.

Two basic elements in our health

There are two habits in elderly people's lifestyle which are directly linked to their health: Physical exercise and nutrition.

Physical exercise

Physical exercise, in its many alternatives and personal preferences, is a factor which **may prevent many conditions** associated with old age. Regular, moderate, physical exercise provides an overall sense of wellbeing in those who practice it. It strengthens the heart and the lungs, as well as preventing high blood pressure, osteoporosis, diabetes and heart disease. It maintains supple muscles and joints, and relieves lumbar and arthritic pain (see the box on page 120 containing the highly interesting experience of 101-year old Hulda Crooks).

Physical activity also brings **mental wellbeing**. Tasks which rely on our memory and reasoning improve when we take physical exercise, as does our capacity for concentration and keeping alert. It also forestalls anxiety and depression producing joy and a positive outlook. Lastly, the wellbeing attained through exercise also helps to avoid many accidents.

Physical exercise need not be complicated or associated with costly sports. A *one-hour walk every day is enough* to reap the benefits associated with physical exercise. Keeping up an active life in retirement is one of the secrets of wellbeing and longevity. Below we have some advice which may assist you in keeping active:

- Busy yourself with *household projects*. Work in your flower or vegetable garden.
- Accept **responsibilities** which oblige you *to go back and forth and to walk.*
- Take the *stairs* instead of the elevator, always holding firmly to the handrail.
- Wear *comfortable clothes and rubber-soled sports shoes* to walk comfortably without running the risk of falling.

- Adjust your life to the *solar clock*. Keep yourself active during the day and sleep at night. You will perform better if you are in parallel with the natural day.
- Seek out moments of peace and quiet on a daily basis, *to meditate, pray or listen to relaxing music*. The beginning of the day or nightfall can be the ideal time for these activities.

Balanced nutrition

Balanced nutrition is of utmost importance for the health of elderly people. Unfortunately, changes in old age make us abandon many of the good habits of a pleasant and varied diet. Be it due to loss of smell and taste, the loss of teeth or because of living alone without the motivation to cook for themselves, many elderly people end up eating poorly.

Today, it is known that nutrition is closely related to health and the aging process. For example, it is common to find elderly people with **vitamin and mineral** deficiencies (especially vitamin E, and minerals such as magnesium and calcium). There are also diseases directly derived from the excessive consumption of fats, so very common in this day and age.

Nutrition plays an important role in preventing illnesses such as arteriosclerosis, heart disease and diabetes. Certain vitamin deficiencies have been associated with the loss of mental faculties. For example, a recent study has demonstrated that consumption of **vitamin B6** improves the memory function. It would also seem evident that a deficiency of **vitamin D** may lead to hip fractures in old people.

HOW TO KEEP OUR BONES HEALTHY

The following measures contribute to the strengthening of our bones in general and preventing osteoporosis:

- **Adhere to a diet rich in calcium**. Regularly consume products rich in calcium: low-fat dairy products (skimmed milk, yogurt, fresh cheese …), green leaf vegetables (chard, spinach …), sesame seeds and wholemeal cereals.
But beware! There are foods that contribute to a loss in calcium; by consuming them, any attempt at building up calcium reserves will be of little or no use. These foods are: Animal proteins (all types of meat), coffee, salt and phosphorous (present in fizzy drinks). Abstain from eating these products or eat them in very small quantities.

- **Ensure an adequate intake of vitamin D**. Egg yolk, fish and cod liver oil all contain this vitamin. However, even without consuming these foods one can still get enough vitamin D by going out into the fresh air and receiving a moderate amount of sunrays directly on the skin (10-15 minutes a day are enough). The human organism converts cholesterol into vitamin D within the skin.

- **Take regular, moderate physical exercise**. Walk every day. This is the best exercise for elderly people. When you walk you are not only strengthening your skeleton and muscles but also your motor coordination which can help to prevent accidents.

- **Do not smoke**. Among the many negative effects of smoking is that it contributes to a greater loss in bone density.

At all times the possibility of **falls should be avoided**:

- ✓ Keep the floor free from sliding rugs, cords or dust and dirt which could make you slip.
- ✓ Stairs should be well lit. Use the handrail when going up and down.
- ✓ Use comfortable, rubber-soled shoes.
- ✓ Place objects you use often within hands' reach.
- ✓ Use a permanent safety handrail in the bath or shower.

Furthermore, the regular consumption of fresh fruit and vegetables, especially citrus fruits and green leafy vegetables, reduces the risk of cerebral stroke. The unit entitled "A Guide to nutrition in old age", on page 119, contains dietary advice for elderly readers.

Osteoporosis

Another relatively common problem is osteoporosis. It affects millions of elderly men and women in our country and neighboring nations.

What is osteoporosis? The human skeleton, far from being an inert material, is a live tissue which reacts positively when it is stimulated with physical exercise or adequate nutrients.

In fact, all the bones in a human being are in a state of constant regeneration, eliminating bone cells and replacing them with new ones. A healthy adult skeleton is completely renewed every 8 to 10 years.

As part of our normal physical development, at around the age of 35 our bone tissue loss increases (Merrill, S.S. and Verbrugge, E.L. M., 1999). It is a completely normal process, but replacing this loss makes strong demands on our organism.

In most cases this does not lead to undesirable effects. However, in certain people, replacement of bone tissue does not keep pace with what is being lost.

The result is the onset of osteoporosis, which weakens the skeletal system in general and makes bones weak and susceptible to fracturing.

1. **Eat fresh fruit or vegetables at every meal.** If this is not always possible, use canned or frozen products. The ideal amount is five portions a day.

2. **Eat a small quantity of pulses or nuts every day.** These foods contain proteins which help to repair and restore our organism.

3. **Eat small amounts of fat and sugar.** Foods rich in fat and sugar are tasty, but provide too many calories and no other nutrients.

4. **Aim to include bread, potatoes, rice or pasta in every meal.** They represent our body's preferred source of energy.

5. **Include calcium-rich foods** such as milk, yogurt, fresh cheese and green-leaved vegetables in your daily diet.

6. **Drink liquids every day; one to two liters outside of meals**. Water is the best drink, although you may include some fruit juices, skimmed milk or herbal teas.

7. **Keep to regular** meal times.

8. **Keep an eye on your weight** and consult your doctor if you lose or gain weight without wishing to do so.

9. **Eat brown bread**, wild rice, whole meal pasta and wholemeal cereals. If you suffer from constipation, this may be due to a lack of roughage in your diet.

10. **Ensure that your diet contains enough iron**. Eat spinach, cabbage, lentils, beans and eggs in moderation.

11. **Avoid vitamin D deficiency**. It is contained in eggs and dairy products. Sunlight on our skin stimulates the production of vitamin D.

12. **Eat with moderation** so as not to overload your digestive system.

13. Although you may indulge from time to time, **avoid high-calorie foods such as cakes, biscuits or sweets, which do not provide other nutrients**.

14. **Make meals a pleasant occasion**. Enjoy your partner's company at mealtimes and consider them as special moments. If you live alone, occasionally meet up with a friend for a meal.

119

WHY HULDA CROOKS LIVED EXUDING GOOD HEALTH TO THE AGE OF 101

Hulda Crooks (1896 – 1997) was born in an agricultural region of Saskatchewan (Canada). Her childhood passed helping out with family household duties and going to school when farm-work allowed. On coming of age, she left home to complete a high school education and finally, under great financial hardship, she pursued a degree in nutritional studies. At the age of 31 she married Sam Crooks, a companion from university, and the couple had a son.

Hulda went into a career as a dietary research assistant at Loma Linda University in California.

From her youth Hulda suffered from **anemia, nervousness** and almost permanent **tiredness**.

Encouraged by her husband, *at the age of 54* she began to exercise her muscles by walking up hills and mountains. The state of wellbeing she found encouraged her to continue until, at the age of 66 and then widowed, she climbed Mount Whitney (4,418 m) for the first time.

For the following 25 years Hulda Crooks would climb the mountain every year until she was 91, thus being the oldest person capable of reaching the summit of Mount Whitney.

That same year she was invited to Japan to climb Mount Fujiyama. On crowning this peak, she also became the oldest person ever to have climbed it. The Japanese, with their great respect for old age, paid great homage to her, holding celebrations and affectionately calling her "Grandma Fuji".

Apart from these two famous peaks, Hulda climbed many mountains, her most active period being *between the ages of 81 and 91*. From the age of 91 she continued taking regular physical exercise but she no longer climbed to high summits. She lived healthfully until she passed away peacefully at the age of 101.

What was the secret of her vitality and longevity?

- Her marriage was a great source of **emotional support**, her husband being a highly beneficial influence for her.
- When she was 54 years old she made the firm decision **not to let her** depressive feelings overcome her.
- She also decided to **exercise** by regularly going mountaineering.
- Upon her retirement Hulda took great care with her **diet**, eating only fruit, cereals, pulses, vegetables, a little milk and one or two eggs a week.
- She **renounced** tea, coffee and any soft drink containing caffeine.
- She *ate twice a day*.
- She got up and went to bed **early**.
- Furthermore, Hulda accepted Jesus Christ as her Savior and followed his teachings, the practice of which enabled her **to find peace** with herself and have extraordinary relations with other people until the day she died. She passed away with the conviction of her own resurrection after death.

Source: *Grandma Whitney*, from William C. Andress.

Photographs of Hulda Crooks by courtesy of William C. Andress.

The loss of the one who shared decades of joys and sorrows is one of the most traumatic events which a person may face. The loss of a loved one may produce pain, sadness and anguish for months afterwards. Furthermore, this usually happens when one's children are living independently and one's brothers and sisters are getting on in years, thus complicating the process. Despite all this, there are ways of preparing oneself to face this difficult stage. The following paragraphs are **aimed at preparing for** this moment, at understanding the process and at enabling you to successfully come through it.

Firstly, everyone needs to be aware of the **process of grieving** which one experiences at the loss of a loved one. Despite the difficulty of the situation, it is a universal process which almost everyone passes through. The box on the next page outlines the typical phases a widow/er will undergo.

Another area of preparation involves **one's self-confidence**. There are people who believe that if their spouse dies, they will be unable to overcome their grief. It is true that some risks, such as depression, are entailed. However, this is a minor risk and it can be cured even in those cases where it does occur. Research shows that mature people have more resources to face the loss of a loved one than younger people do (Digiulio, J.F., 1992). And this is definitely something which should bolster one's self-confidence.

It is useful to work together in building up each other's self-confidence. A mutual **building of self-esteem** is one of the strengths of a good marital relationship. When both spouses have a healthy self-esteem, both will be prepared to survive on their own when the time comes.

Lastly, we must consider **such practical issues** as the financial administration, housework, or relationships with relatives. In traditional marriages, the husband is responsible for bank transactions and other bureaucratic matters; he also takes care of any D.I.Y., travel bookings, etcetera. For her part, the wife tends to be the culinary expert of the two, including the shopping and cooking, as well as maintaining family relations and the cleaning and decoration of the home.

It is **recommended that each one start to learn the other's duties**. Total ignorance in practical aspects is very dangerous. A husband helping his wife with the housework or the wife learning to carry out bureaucratic matters not only provides a challenge to keep faculties active, but also provides a way of communicating mutual affection and support while building skills that may become necessary with the loss of their partner.

One of the first experiences a widow/er **has to face is loneliness**. Being without company may prove overwhelming. The widow/er has to eat alone, sleep alone, watch TV alone … She/he no longer has anyone with whom to share past memories or family anecdotes.

All of this produces a sense of emptiness, an absence of personal worth, generalized weakness and significant mood swings. However, these irregularities do tend to disappear over time. In fact, memories of a spouse, initially obsessive, soon become something pleasant and a source of relief. To all of this

The loss of a spouse: Stages to overcoming the pain

By studying people who have lost a spouse in their old age, a pattern of recovery has been established. An awareness of these stages will help the reader to prepare him/herself for this moment or to successfully overcome it if it has already happened. Knowing that most people successfully pass through the resolution stage in less than a year after the death of a loved one should inspire us with hope.

1. **The shock stage**. This is the most painful moment after the loss of a loved one. The grieving person passes through a state of shock which may show itself as numbness or desperate weeping. During this stage many opt for denial: "He/she can't have died …". It is also frequent to find illogical thoughts ("I'd do anything to have him/her back …"); desperate thoughts ("I wish I could die too"); or anxiety ("I can't survive without him/her"). This stage may last for several weeks during which a person may experience moments of confusion, emptiness, sadness or tearful breakdowns. These symptoms are completely normal and become less frequent and less intense as the days go by.

2. **The transition stage**. This is characterized by memories of the loved one which tend to occupy the bereaved person's thoughts. During this period, the person tends to feel bound by a strong feeling that his/her spouse is present. For the first time the person feels hope of survival and success in the absence of the loved one, and begins to make plans to get back to a normal life. The transition stage lasts about six months.

3. **The resolution stage**. During this stage the necessary adaptations and changes are gradually made, now without a link or dependency on the loved one. It is the moment when the widow or widower shows her/himself and the rest that the crisis has been overcome. As is to be expected, the memory of the deceased continues to be present, sometimes invoking pleasure, other times sadness. Either way, these memories are now free of pain and anguish.

we must add some practical issues, such as a decrease in income or an increase in workload as there is no one to share the duties. It is therefore of the utmost importance to take several simple **measures** such as those outlined below:

- Take **moderate physical exercise** to enhance your organic functions and to regulate your sleep mechanism.
- Eat **light, nutritive meals**.
- **Avoid excesses**. Try not to take on too much, although it is good to keep yourself busy.

- **Speak about your deceased spouse** with a relative or friend. This helps to assimilate the reality of his/her death.
- **Be patient** during the recovery process. As with a physical injury, recovery from the grief over the death of a spouse takes time.
- Care for something or someone. Bereaved people often find refuge in looking after plants or animals (see the box on page 123 about pets).

One in every ten people who are widowed suffer from the full range of symptoms of depression, and women are at significantly greater risk than men. Every depression involves a very significant strong element of loss. Specifically, loss of dignity, loss of employment or the loss of a loved one are typical events which may bring on depressive symptoms.

The most outstanding **symptoms** of depression are: Elated or depressive (low spirited) moods; loss of interest in what is usually funny or pleasurable; weight loss, insomnia, overexcitement or a "slow-down" of motor functions; low self-esteem; lack of concentration; indecisiveness; and thoughts of death.

The grieving process is sometimes accompanied by feelings of **anger and frustration**. In order to combat them, it is necessary **to vent** these feelings. Physical exercise is one of the most effective ways of channeling anger and frustration. As far as your faculties will allow you, take physical exercise. Consult your doctor for advice on your limits. There are people who shout or write their thoughts down to expel their anger. Whatever your style is, it is not good to keep those thoughts inside.

Bereavement also comes to couples whose relationship was problematic or conflictive. This may leave the **surviving spouse with the sensation that he/she will never be able to mend those difficulties**. In these cases it is necessary to think calmly of the good and the bad times in the relationship, accept the past and go confidently and serenely forward. Avoid accusing one's spouse or oneself over past events. Nobody is perfect and most people do the best they can within their personal and social constraints.

Faith and religious beliefs constitute a fundamental pillar of support. In fact, a great lot of people with very little interest in religion return to belief in an attempt to find peace and calmness. The expectation of resurrection at the end of our time is a biblical truth which helps a believer to trust in a better life after death and a re-encounter with his/her loved ones. Bitterness and grief, while undesirable in themselves, may encourage people to reaffirm their hope and strengthen their faith.

PETS: GOOD COLLABORATORS

A dog, a cat or a bird can often offer the necessary loyalty and affection to make an elderly person happier, especially at the sadder times. Studies on physical and mental health have shown that pets prevent stress and keep our blood pressure within desirable levels.

Elderly people with a pet at home find themselves under the positive obligation to get up in the morning to attend to the animal's walks, feeding or care. In doing so, they are also attending to their own physical and psychological needs.

Depression can be cured

The loss of a loved one almost always involves feelings of loneliness, sadness or anguish. This does not imply clinical depression. However, sometimes a person falls into clinical or major depression with several of the symptoms outlined in the text, which may last for weeks or longer. It is estimated that depression strikes one in every ten cases of widowhood. Depression has a good prognosis if professionally treated using drugs and psychotherapy. The psychotherapeutic advice in this chapter is the basis for *self-help in fighting depression caused by the bereavement of a loved one*.

- **Speak to someone you trust**. Seek out a friend or relative you value and who understands you, and talk to them. Brooding on your own about the loss of a loved one will not make the symptoms go away.

- **Keep yourself active**. Walk in the fresh air, do errands or some "do-it-yourself" activity. This can help to keep you occupied while the period of grief passes.

- **Eat properly**. Even if you have no appetite, eat a small amount of vegetables, fresh fruit, cereals and pulses. It is important to keep your body nourished.

- **Do not become obsessed with insomnia**. As we get older, we do not need so much sleep. When you cannot sleep, do not become irritated. Make yourself comfortable on the sofa and read a good book or listen to the radio. This will help you to relax and finally fall asleep.

- **Think on the good side of things**. It is difficult but not impossible to think positively in the midst of depressive feelings. Get together with positive people and keep away from pessimists.

- **Look after your self-esteem**. Try not to blame yourself and avoid feelings of inferiority. If you have done something wrong, ask the offended person for forgiveness; if this is not possible because that person is no longer alive, ask God sincerely for forgiveness. Your state of mind will make a surprising recovery.

- **Adopt a hopeful attitude**. Hope is a human need. Without it we easily fall into doubt, fear, anxiety; all experiences associated with depression. If you believe in God, pray with all your heart. Prayer is an important factor in bringing hope and wellbeing.

A purely biological analysis of human life and death is incomplete. Birth, growth, death … isn't there anything else? Human existence, with its achievements and satisfactions, but also with its suffering and injustice, needs a purpose. What we can see at the moment has, necessarily, to be part of a greater picture, of a global plan of everlasting existence.

Cultures around the world resort to hope beyond the tomb. In the Judeo-Christian tradition, the process revealed in the Scriptures is quite simple, and perhaps for that reason, it is sometimes rejected:

1. Since evil entered the Universe, there has been a **constant conflict between good and evil**.

2. In his infinite wisdom, God has allowed evil to develop until **its negative** consequences are clearly revealed.

3. In his love, God laid out a plan to save humanity.

This plan involves eliminating everything which makes us unhappy: Pain, disease, deterioration, death …

4. The results of this plan will be seen at the end of time, when the dead **are resurrected** and a new world is created. In the last book of the Bible, Someone who never lies announces "*a new Heaven and a new Earth*". In that society "*there will no longer be death, nor weeping, nor lamentations, nor pain, because all that existed no longer exists*". You can find these promises in the Bible last book, Revelation. There we are told how God will restore planet Earth to the same condition He Himself gave it on Creation. There will no longer be physical deterioration; people will recover their strength. In summary, we will be young again!

It is for this very reason that believers face death with hope. Because God has promised to give us another opportunity to be happy.

ACCEPTING THE PAST AND TRUSTING IN THE FUTURE ... BECAUSE THERE IS A FUTURE!

In a study carried out by Koenig and his associates (Koenig, H. G., George, L. K., and Siegler, I. C., 1988) they asked a sample of men and women aged between 55 and 80 to look back over their lives and to identify their worst experiences. After that they were asked to explain how they had confronted these events. The most common reply was: "By embracing religion," followed in importance by "keeping myself busy," "turning to my family and friends," etc.

In another study, also led by Koenig (Koenig, H. G., Kevale, J. N., and Ferrel, C., 1988), it was confirmed that the subjects with the best state of mind and most positive attitudes towards getting old and dying enjoyed one or more of the following **religious activities:**

- **Organized** activity (attending and participating in religious services).
- **Informal** activity (praying to God and reading the Bible in private).
- **Spiritual** activity (firmly believing in a set of doctrines and principles).

Those who contemplate their past with disappointment and dissatisfaction and concentrate on the negative events in their lives tend to experience greater levels of fear and uncertainty about death. Meanwhile those who look on the past with a sense of **acceptance** of both the good and the bad and concentrate specifically on the **positive events** contemplate death with serenity and confidence.

We recommend taking a serene look at one's personal history, contemplating it as a **gift from God**, a unique and marvelous experience which leads towards a temporary end, but which then allows us to place ourselves in God's hands; He who gave us life and now calls us to rest. In this way we may experience **hope** of that day when the dead will be resurrected in Christ to always be with the Lord (see Paul's First Epistle to the Thessalonians, chapter 4, verses 16 and 17).

We suggest turning to God as early as possible. Many have never worried about this supernatural dimension, which is so important for a human being. But it is never too late. Accept God, speak to Him, tell Him your doubts and your heartaches, and also of your joys. You will see how hope is born inside you and you will understand how you too can be saved and live eternally ... young! Try it.

ADES, P. A., BALLOR, D. L., ASHIKAGA, T., UTTON, J. L., y NAIR, K. S., "Weight training improves walking endurance in healthy elderly persons." *Annals of Internal Medicine* 124:568-572, 1996.

ALPERN, D. M., "It scares the hell out of me." *Newsweek* 14 de marzo: 44, 1988.

AMERICAN COUNCIL ON SCIENCE AND HEALTH., "Premenstrual Syndrome". Summit (Nueva Jersey): ACSH, 1985.

BOHANNAN, P., "The six stations of divorce", en BOHANNAN, P., *Divorce and After*. Nueva York: Doubleday, 1970.

BORCHERDT, B., *You Can Control Your Feelings: 24 Guides to Emotional Self-control*. Sarasota (Florida): Professional Resource Press, 1993.

Bremner, W. J., Vitiello, M. V., y Prinz, P. N., "Loss of circadian rhythmicity in blood testosterone levels with aging in normal men". *Journal of Clinical Endocrinology and Metabolism* 56:1278-1281, 1983.

BUCHANAN, C. M., MACCOBY, E. E. y DORNBUSCH, S. M., *Adolescents After Divorce*. Cambridge (Massachusetts): Harvard University Press, 1996.

CROSBY, J. F., *Illusion and Disillusion: The Self in Love and Marriage*. Belmont (California): Wadsworth, 1991.

DEFRAIN, J., "Androgynous parents outline their needs". *Family Coordinator* abril: 237-243, 1979.

DIGIULIO, J. F., "Early widowhood: An atypical transition". *Journal of Mental Health Counseling* 14:97-109, 1992.

ERIKSON, E. H., *Childhood and Society*. Nueva York: Norton, 1950.

FIATARONE, M. A., MARKS, E. C., RYAN, N. D., MEREDITH, C. N., LIPSITZ, L. A. y EVANS, W. J., "High-intensity strength training in nonagenarians: Effects on skeletal muscles". *Journal of the American Medical Association* 263:3029-3034, 1990.

FIATARONE, M. A., O'NEILL, E. F. y RYAN, N. D., "Exercise training and nutritional supplementation for physical frailty in very elderly people". *New England Journal of Medicine* 330:1769-1775, 1994.

FISHER, L., *The American Association of Retired Persons (AARP)/Modern Maturity Study*. Washington D.C.: AARP, 1999.

FOWERS, B. J. y OLSON, D. H., "Predicting marital success with PREPARE: A predictive validity study". *Journal of Marital and Family Therapy* 12:403-413, 1986.

FRAGA, C. G., ET AL., "Ascorbic acid protects against endogenous oxidative DNA damage in human sperm". *Proceedings of the National Academy of Sciences of the United States of America* 88:11003-11006, 1991.

GELLES, R. J., *Intimate Violence in Families*. Beverly Hills (California): Sage, 1997.

GOULD, R. L., "Adult life stages: Growth towards self-tolerance". *Psychology Today* agosto: 74-78, 1975.

GOULD, R.L., "Transformational tasks in adulthood", en POLLOCK, G. H. y GREENSPAN, S. I. (Eds.), *The Course of Life: Vol. 6 Late Adulthood*. Madison (Connecticut): International University Press, 1993.

GOULD, R. L., *Transformations: Growth and Change in Adult Life*. Nueva York: Simon & Schuster, 1979.

HARLEY, W. F., *His Needs, Her Needs*. Grand Rapids (Michigan): Revell, 1986.

HAYES, M. P., "Strengthening marriage in the middle years", en STINNET, N., CHESSER, B. y DEFRAIN, J. (Eds.), *Building Family Strengths: Blueprints For Action*. Lincoln (Nebraska): University of Nebraska Press, 1979.

KERCKHOFF, A. C. y DAVIS, K. E., "Value consensus and need complementarity in mate selection". *American Sociological Review* 27:295-303, 1962.

KILMANN, R. y THOMAS, K., "Interpersonal conflict: Handling behavior as reflections of Jungian personality dimensions". *Psychological Reports* 37:971-980, 1975.

KOENIG, H. G., GEORGE, L. K., y SIEGLER, I. C., "The use of religion and other emotion-regulating coping strategies among older adults". *The Gerontologist* 28(3):303-310,1988.

KOENIG, H. G., KEVALE, J. N., y FERREL, C., "Religion and well-being in later life". *The Gerontologist* 28(1):18-28,1988.

KRUTTSCHNITT, C., HEATH, L. y WARD, D. A., "Family violence, television viewing habits, and other adolescent experiences related to violent criminal behavior". *Criminology* 24(2):235-26,1986.

LARSEN, A. S. y OLSON, D. H., "Predicting marital satisfaction using PREPARE: A replication study". *Journal of Marital and Family Therapy* 15:311-322, 1989.

LESTER, R. y VAN THEIL, D. H., "Gonadal function in chronic alcoholic men". *Advances in Experimental Medicine and Biology* 85A:339-414, 1977.

MASTERS, W. H. y JOHNSON, V. E., *Human Sexual Response*. Boston (Massachusetts): Little Brown & Co., 1966.

McCARTNEY, N., HICKS, A. L., MARTIN, J. y WEBBER, C. E., "A longitudinal trial of weight training in the elderly: Continued improvements in year 2". *The Journals of Gerontology: Series A: Biological Sciences and Medical Sciences* 51:425-433, 1996.

McGOLDRICK, M. y PRETO, N. G., "Ethnic intermarriage: Implications for therapy". *Family Process* 23:347-367, 1984.

McLANAHAN, S. y SANDEFUR, G., *Growing Up With a Single Parent: What Hurts, What Helps*. Cambridge (Massachusetts): Harvard University Press, 1994.

MERRILL, S. S. y VERBRUGGE, L. M., "Health and disease in midlife", en WILLIS, S. y REID, J. D. (Eds.), *Life in the Middle: Psychological and Social Development in Middle Age*. San Diego: Academic Press, 1999.

MILLER, S. y MILLER, P. A., *Core Communications: Skills and Processes*. Littleton (Colorado): Interpersonal Communication Programs, 1991.

MOORE, K. A., "What a difference a dad makes". *Child Trends Report*. Washington DC: Child Trends, 1998.

MURSTEIN, B. I., "A classification and extension of the SVR theory of dyadic pairing". *Journal of Marriage and the Family* 42:777-792, 1987.

National Institute on Aging (NIA), *Senility: Myth or madness*. Washington, DC: U.S. Government Printing Office, 1980.

NATIONAL OPINION RESEARCH CENTER, *Survey on Sexual Behavior*. Storrs (Connecticut): Roper Center for Public Opinion Research, 1994.

OLSON, D. H. y DEFRAIN, J., *Marriage and the Family. Diversity and Strengths*. Mountain View (California): Mayfield Publishing Company, 2000.

OLSON, D. H., FYE, S. y OLSON A., *National Survey of Happy and Unhappy Married Couples*. Minneapolis (Minnesota): Life Innovations, 1999.

ORBUCH, T. L. ET AL., "Marital quality through the life course". *Social Psychology Quarterly* 59(2):162-171, 1996.

PARROTT, L. y PARROTT, L., *Saving Your Marriage Before it Starts*. Grand Rapids (Michigan): Zondervan Publishing House, 1996.

PEREYRA, M., *Psicología del perdón*. Santiago de Chile: Publica Impresores Ltda., 1993.

POWELL, J., *The Secret of Staying in Love*. Valencia (California): 1974.

RISMAN, B.J. y JOHNSON-SUMERFORD, D., "Doing it fairly: A study of postgender marriages". *Journal of Marriage and the Family* 60:23-40, 1998.

SCHWARTZ, P., *Love Between Equals: How Peer Marriage Really Works*. Nueva York: Free Press, 1995.

STEINMETZ, S. K., "Family violence", en SUSSMAN, M. B. y STEINMETZ, S. K. (Eds.), *Handbook of Marriage and the Family*. Nueva York: Plenum, 1987.

STINNETT, N., STINNETT, N., DEFRAIN, J. y DEFRAIN, N., *New Families*. Nueva York: Doubleday, 1997.

VAN PELT, N. L., *Highly Effective Marriage*. Hagerstown (Maryland): Review and Herald Publishing Association, 2000.

WALLERSTEIN, J. S. y BLAKESLEE, S., *Second Chances: Men, Women, and Children a Decade After Divorce*. Nueva York: Ticknor & Fields, 1996.

WALLHAGEN, M.I., ET AL., "An increasing prevalence of hearing impairment and associated risk factors over three decades of the Alameda County Study". *American Journal of Public Health* 87(3):440-442, 1997.

WHISMAN, M. A., DIXON, A. E. y JOHNSON, B., "Therapists' perspectives of couple problems and treatment issues in couple therapy". *Journal of Family Psychology* 11(3):361-366, 1998.

WOODWARD, J. C., *The Solitude of Loneliness*. Lexington (Massachusetts): Lexington Books/Heath, 1988.

WURTMAN, R. J. y WURTMAN, J. J., "Carbohydrates and depression". *Scientific American* 260 (1):68-75.

BOOKS IN THIS COLLECTION

Foods that Heal
Dr. George D. Pamplona-Roger

You can change your life by changing your diet. You will discover foods that help you avoid weight gain. Foods that help you breathe more freely. Foods that help you digest. Foods that battle infection. Foods that benefit the skin, muscles, urinary tract, intestine, stomach, liver, lungs, blood, arteries, heart, nerves, and eyes.

Plants that Heal
Dr. George D. Pamplona-Roger

Most people in the world get their medicine from field and forest. Now you can too, thanks to this treasury of valuable information about nature's pharmacy. Full of gorgeous photography, this book unlocks the secrets of the rich tradition of natural remedies–plants that heal the body and invigorate the mind.

Steps to Happiness

STEPS TO HAPPINESS is an inspiring book unlike any other. It is small, but thought-provoking; simple but captivating. Its main benefit is that it shows us the way towards a person who can understand us in a way that no one else can, and like no one else, he seeks us and wants to welcome us to himself. Once you know him, you will understand why he is "the way" to happiness.

A Future of Hope

These eleven chapters are simple, yet thoughtprovoking. They cover topics of great interest, such as why we suff er, true peace, life after death, and the fi nal victory of God's love. With a focus on a global crisis that impacts all of humanity, it off ers a happy ending for those who trust in God's love.

Safeliz

Request today further information from:

EDITORIAL SAFELIZ, S.L.
Pradillo, 6 · Pol. Ind. La Mina
E-28770 · Colmenar Viejo, Madrid, Spain
Tel.: [+34] 91 845 98 77 · Fax: [+34] 91 845 98 65
admin@safeliz.com · www.safeliz.com

Happy Couples
Dr. Julián Melgosa y Anette Melgosa

The problems a couple face are not the same when they are going out together, when they have children or when they become elderly. This is a practical book that can accompany us throughout life's journey because it encompasses a couple's entire life together, from courtship to old age.